Localizing Employee Communications
A Handbook

Ray Walsh

Localizing Employee Communications
A Handbook
Copyright © 2020 Ray Walsh

All rights reserved. No part of this book may be reproduced or transmitted in any form or by any means without the prior written permission of the copyright holder, except for the inclusion of brief quotations in a review.

Disclaimer

The information in this book is provided on an "as is" basis, without warranty. While every effort has been taken by the author and XML Press in the preparation of this book, the author and XML Press shall have neither liability nor responsibility to any person or entity with respect to any loss or damages arising from the information contained herein.

This book contains links to third-party web sites that are not under the control of the author or XML Press. The author and XML Press are not responsible for the content of any linked site. Inclusion of a link in this book does not imply that the author or XML Press endorses or accepts any responsibility for the content of that third-party site.

Credits

Series Producer and Editor:	Scott Abel
Series Cover Design:	Marc Posch
Publisher:	Richard Hamilton
Figure 1.1	Photo by Emile Guillemot on Unsplash
Figure 2.3	Illustration by gienlee

Trademarks

XML Press and the XML Press logo are trademarks of XML Press.

All terms mentioned in this book that are known to be trademarks or service marks have been capitalized as appropriate. Use of a term in this book should not be regarded as affecting the validity of any trademark or service mark.

XML Press
Laguna Hills, California
http://xmlpress.net

First Edition
ISBN: 978-1-937434-66-3 (print)
ISBN: 978-1-937434-67-0 (ebook)

Table of Contents

Foreword vii
Preface ix
    Specialized terminology xiv
    Interviews xv
    Acknowledgements xv

I. The Landscape In Country 1

  1. The Challenges of Communicating Globally 3
      Declaring English your corporate language is not a solution 4
      Most messages are forgettable 5
      English-language read rates 7
      Translation, localization, and co-creation 8
      Employee engagement and the influence of communications 10
      The myth of the information cascade 11
      How local businesses distort your message 13
      Mission and vision versus profit and loss 15
      US content that thinks it's global 16
  2. The Context for Local and Global Content 19
      Cluster one: locally generated content 21
      Cluster two: corporate-generated content 22
      Cluster three: global/local hybrid content 24
      Graphing your employee deliverables 25
      Measuring international communications 26
      Collecting quantitative data: local considerations 26
      Collecting qualitative data: avoiding distortion 28
      Technology barriers to internal communication 30
      Reaching the non-employee workforce 31
  3. Translation Challenges 35
      Originals and translations are not identical 35
      The problem of bad business writing 37
      The true costs of translating content internally 39
  4. Visual Communication 43
      Limitations of visual communication 44
      Managing photography 44
      Managing graphics 46
      Managing video 47

5. Local Communicators 51
    Resource capabilities in small, medium, and large markets 53
    Common network skills and limitations 54
    Listen to your major markets 55
    Conclusion 56

II. Leadership, Governance, and Budget 57

6. Setting the Stage 59
    The struggle for resources 59
    Justifying the need for localization 60
    Finding a leader 62
    Reporting lines for global communication teams 63
    Evaluating costs, benefits, and who pays 64
    What managers need to understand about communicating globally 67
    Tying localization to business outcomes 68
    Imagining a better intranet 69
    Intranet measurement 73

7. Localization Models 77
    Centrally managed teams with limited flexibility 78
    Centrally managed teams with greater flexibility 81
    Autonomous teams with strong guidance 85
    Autonomous teams with minimal guidance 87
    Putting the models together 89
    Conclusion 92

III. Low- and No-Cost Strategies 93

8. Preparing for Localization 95
    What headquarters and local businesses can learn from each other 96
    The role of local business units in localization 97
    Localization 101: budgeting time for in-country review 101
    Where English can be effective 103
    Inform in English, persuade in local language 103
    Targeted campaign briefings 105

9. Managing Translation 109
    Learn when and how your company translates 109
    The dangers of skimping on translation 110
    Assessing and prioritizing costs for translations 110
    Why you need plain language 117
    Providing machine translations 119
    Using style guides for better translations 121
    English outside the Anglo-American world 123

10. Making Visuals More Adaptable 125
    Connecting designers with users 125
    Co-creating with templates and brand guidelines 127
    Balancing fixed and flexible brand elements 128
    Creating and maintaining a design system language 129
    Localizing with templates and guidelines 130
    Conclusion 133

IV. Capabilities and Resources 135

11. Thinking Internationally 137
    The international mindset 138
    Global conference calls 139
    Using agencies to generate content 141
    Insourced or outsourced, prepare a briefing 145
12. Photography, Video, and Digital Signage 147
    Image vacuums and lawsuit risks 149
    Operations and images 152
    The limits of a photo library 152
    All digital signage is local 154
13. Leveraging Content from Other Groups 159
    Measuring localized content 160
    Finding and supporting brand champions 164
    Socializing marketing content 166
14. Tapping into Social Media 169
    Working with social media teams 170
15. Building a Better Team 173
    Culture is in the break room 173
    Better network, better outcomes 175
    Give your network what they need 176
    Developing general communications skills 180
    Sustaining global execution 181
16. Working with Your Network 183
    Thinking like a communicator 184
    Encouraging honest discussion 187
    Getting the network in touch with the business 188
    Content development that builds relationships 189
    Team purpose and postmortems 191
    Content that both corporate and local communicators get wrong 192
17. Developing Your Network 197
    Group meetings 197
    Values-driven workshops 202

Table of Contents

    Collaborating through problems 202
    Career development for creative teams 204
    Conclusion 205
18. Afterword 207
Interviewee Biographies 211
    Arlene Birt 211
    Deborah S. Bosley 211
    Dr. Barbara Gibson 211
    Rosie Halfhead 211
    John Kohl 212
    Prof. Élise LeMoing Maas 212
    Sean Matthews 212
    Gerry McGovern 213
    Mark Ohlsen 213
    Alan Oram 213
    Jonathan Phillips 213
    Alan J. Porter 214
    Leonard Rau 214
    Ann Rockley 214
    Carmen Simon 215
    Val Swisher 215
References and Further Reading 217
Glossary 223
Index 233

Foreword

by Val Swisher, CEO Content Rules, Inc.

It's been a handful of years since my book, *Global Content Strategy: A Primer,* was released by XML Press. Since that time, the world has become smaller and more interconnected. And without a doubt, more companies translate more content into more languages every year.

The reason for the rise in translation is two-fold. First, to attract and keep global customers, most companies recognize that they must deliver content in the language of the customer. It is no longer a "nice to have." Translation and localization of product information is a competitive imperative.

The second reason for the rise in translation is that the technologies used in the translation process have improved. Machine translation, once a hit-or-miss set of rules and statistics, is well on its way to becoming just as good as (and possibly more consistent than) human translation. More language services providers (LSPs) offer neural machine translation (NMT) solutions. And these artificial intelligence-based, machine learning enabled systems do a significantly better job than any previous algorithm that we've tried.

Even the smallest companies are realizing—and meeting—the demanding to translate product content. Product content includes the usual suspects:

- Sales and marketing materials
- User interface
- Documentation
- Training
- Knowledge base

But what about employee communications?

Unfortunately, employee communications, the internal content that the corporate headquarters shares with employees worldwide, seems to be stuck in the dark English ages.

In his book, *Localizing Employee Communications: A Handbook,* Ray Walsh explores the need for localizing and transcreating the final corporate content frontier. Ray makes a compelling case about the importance of providing corporate communication in local languages. After all, how can we boast about having a global team if we don't even bother to communicate important information in the language that each employee speaks?

The global job market is competitive. Companies vie to hire top talent all over the world. And once onboard, companies need to remain competitive to keep those employees from moving on to other, more compelling jobs.

One of the best ways to truly bond with your global teams is to provide information to them in their language(s). If you want your messages to be read, if you want your global team to function as a single company, then you must think globally and act locally. That is, consider your enterprise as a whole and provide content that is relevant in terms of words, imagery, and design to each locale.

In this book, Ray provides all the reasons to localize corporate communication. He discusses how to get buy-in for the localization effort. He discusses how to create content that can be localized. And he details how to manage the translation effort. This book is a true handbook on the who, what, where, why, and how of corporate communication.

Ray certainly understands the space and makes an eloquent case. But he does not do it alone. Instead, this book draws from numerous interviews, additional books, webinars, industry reports, even PhD theses to provide a comprehensive compendium backed by dozens of industry professionals.

If your company has locations worldwide, this handbook will provide you with invaluable information that will improve communication, morale, productivity, and dare I say, sales. As Ray describes, the money you spend on localizing internal communication will more than pay off in employee engagement, retention, and evangelism.

Preface

Residents in the Ivory Tower are easily duped.

No matter where they go, upper managers are greeted in high-quality English. Their conference calls rarely suffer big language barriers. Their email messages go around the world and replies come back in English.

This proficiency convinces them that the entire organization speaks English well enough and that internal corporate communications don't have to deal with language barriers.

This attitude is symbolized in one stock photo I regularly see—the image of someone shouting into a bullhorn. To me it implies, "we think this is important" or "help us amplify this message." But outside of these photos, bullhorns are used only by riot police and carnival barkers, and the burst of static when they're first turned on is annoying.

Corporate content's use of a bullhorn image is appropriate. The head office is used to broadcasting, and it's a habit that dies hard. Even though we're deeply into an era of social media and user-generated content, we still cling to traditional processes of centralized, command-and-control, send-and-receive channels. Corporate Communication departments are capable of creating good content, but it's just not getting through. It's time that we acknowledged this.

Many leaders in internal communications say practitioners should be less concerned with their stuff—magazines, newsletters, and online content—and more focused on equipping and

> It's time for Corporate Communications to quiet down.

training local managers and ambassadors to make messages more relevant. I come from a background in creating content (before it was called that), but after years of living outside my native US, I'm convinced those leaders are right. It's time for Corporate Communications to quiet down.

We can shake our fists, gnash our teeth, and insist that reading corporate content is part of every employee's job. But that won't solve anything. We need to acknowledge that unless we change our communication practices, only a fraction of our internal audience will pay attention.

If you're frustrated that messages don't travel well or that procedures aren't consistently followed, this book is for you. Whether you create global content from a central vantage point at headquarters or have responsibility for content in your local market, this book will show you how to bridge the gap between corporate and local experience.

Most of the examples I use come from companies headquartered in the Anglosphere,[1] but the tension between the corporate headquarters and the regional offices is common to global companies everywhere.

Corporate content often gets crafted at headquarters, close to decision-makers. The closer to the corporate nucleus that content originates, the more time-consuming the input: meetings, iterations, and round after round of approvals. Getting agreement from all stakeholders takes time; we've all seen documents titled FINAL and FINALFINAL. At the last minute we get the go ahead, and we rush it out the door—in English—and hope for the best.

Rarely do we get the chance to genuinely collaborate with colleagues abroad, so it's easy to be out of touch with their environment and the difficulties they have using the collateral we produce.

I've been working in communications in Europe since 2007, and I found this book necessary for two reasons.

First, my colleagues and clients in the English-speaking world know that linguistic and cultural differences exist, but they have a hard time knowing what to do about them. Time after time, when I bring up a specific challenge a country or group of countries has in delivering a piece of corporate content, they're surprised. "That's interesting," they say, "I never thought of that." But then nothing changes. This book documents some of the organ-

---

[1] The Anglosphere is a group of English-speaking nations that share common cultural and historical ties to the United Kingdom (© 2019 Wikipedia CC BY-SA 3.0).

izational challenges that impede communicating globally and then proposes solutions, some of which are simple practices that any company can do.

Second, no matter how aware I am of difficulties with cross-border communications, I need to remind myself constantly of those barriers to avoid my own well-intentioned mistakes. Global awareness needs constant maintenance.

The first time I realized our Ivory Tower, English-language content wasn't doing everything that I had hoped, I was working in Germany. I'd been brought midstream into a re-branding project. The company sold thousands of products across Europe, and they had country-specific print catalogs and websites. The *brand* was well established across Europe.

They were preparing to evolve each country's catalog and online shop away from their old-school style, which was text- and spec-heavy, and toward something more contemporary with conversational writing and a focus on customer needs. It was a big departure.

They hired a handful of native English speakers like me for the first wave of content creation. The copy we produced was to have two purposes. It would be deployed in the UK as local content, and it would then serve as a model for the company's in-house copy writers across Europe.

It made sense to me. Since their European writers were experienced, familiar with the products, and fluent in English, I expected them to adapt our content easily. The writers I met saw a mountain of work ahead, but they were looking forward to a more creative approach. We had a writer from the UK join our team, but we didn't think to include any of the other European writers.

Once we completed a first wave of new content, I had the chance to sit down with the writer in Germany. I thought our content was familiar in tone, clever and on point, and I was looking forward to a positive review. But I didn't get one.

"To be honest," she said, "sometimes I don't understand it.'

My heart sank as I realized that jokes you have to explain aren't funny. Our content wasn't working. While our European writers sat waiting for input they could use, we had wasted a valuable opportunity. Instead of leveraging an extended team more than twice our size, we had focused all our energy on exquisite, finely tuned English masters, arrogantly assuming that our narrowly focused, UK-centric content would translate easily. We'd underestimated what these experienced writers could do.

That missed opportunity still hurts. I have since worked on many projects where I would have loved to have so many writers on staff. That disappointing conversation was the first of many that showed me why translation doesn't always work, and even though I didn't know the word at the time, it was my first glimpse into what localization might look like.

I now realize that had we collaborated with the remote writers, they could have been creating content simultaneously. That clearly would have been the better choice, since we had a huge volume of work ahead of us. Later, the company scaled back the rebranding, and I can't help but think that because we produced only a few examples, the decision-makers couldn't envision the brand fully implemented. More examples of the new content in more languages would have made a stronger case.

No matter how global our mindsets, we forget to anticipate how our work will be adapted by non-native English speakers. It doesn't help that for many of us, working in another language is something we can only imagine. Even professionals sensitive to language barriers don't always appreciate the process of translation and localization or how routine corporate practices can frustrate our English-speaking, non-native colleagues.

This book argues in favor of an organization that translates almost nothing, where nearly every piece of content is created and deployed locally with only back-end support from global headquarters. Enabling local resources to become the messenger will take a shift in corporate mindset. It means giving up on producing content for worldwide audiences—audiences we mistakenly think of as homogenous. It requires an investment in people and processes that cannot happen overnight. But if you want messaging to be relevant, if you want employees to deliver a similar experience to customers across channels and geographies, and if you want higher retention and more engagement, you need to stop broadcasting globally and go local.

In this book I focus mostly on the people issues related to employee communications. I focused on people and processes because tools for translation and collaboration are evolving so fast that they'll be ready for localized communications long before corporate communicators are.

Several of the experts I interviewed in researching this book emphasized the importance of having skilled people in the right places. Getting things right—or missing the mark entirely—is a question of human intervention. To evolve communications to something more powerful, you must focus on the people who execute it locally, in regional offices, and at headquarters.

Part I of this book outlines the realities your colleagues overseas deal with. Part II examines organizational aspects you need to consider prior to starting a localization program. Part III describes practices that can achieve better outcomes, even with little to no additional budget. Part IV looks at how to manage an autonomous international team of communicators.

Every company has its own international footprint. I sketch out challenges and opportunities you need to consider, but ultimately, your localization strategy and tactics will be unique. I hope this book helps you recognize some of the realities that challenge a company's declaration of unity.

The old saying goes, write what you know. My experience with global companies has been with those based in the US and in Europe. I'm a writer, and fully localizing employee communications touches on topics that are outside of my expertise. When it comes to subjects where I'm in over my head—like working with design guidelines, neuroscience, or automated translation tools—I'll point you to more informed sources. In researching this book, I also came across products that promise solutions to common problems. While I don't always have direct experience with them, I've included references so that you can explore what they have to offer.

Specialized terminology

This book includes a glossary (see Glossary), but a few terms have specialized meanings in the context of employee communications:

content: For employee communications, *content* includes articles, email, social media posts, and tweets, but it can also include speeches, town-hall presentations, management briefings, training materials, photos, videos, podcasts, infographics, and other deliverables produced by what is a jack-of-all-trades profession.

network: Many employee communication managers use the term *network* to describe the people in various countries who help them deliver content to employees. Describing them as a team would sound more likely, but that word doesn't always apply. For many companies, the people doing internal communications have other full-time roles, and their relationship with the Corporate Communications department is more of a loose, voluntary association than a direct reporting line.

Communications versus communications: You will see both Communications (upper-case C) and communications (lower-case c) used throughout this book. With an upper-case C, Communications refers to the departmental function within an organization. With a lower-case c, it's any act of information exchange.

global headquarters, corporate office, and home office: These are some of the names I've heard for the office that serves as the company's main registered postal address. It's the home base for the CEO and other officers, houses most of the global functions, and it's from here that official announcements are distributed. In most cases I use corporate office to refer to what's normally the top of a communications pyramid.

branch office, business units, and profit and loss centers: These are some of the ways companies refer to their disparate locations. These can be variously organized: by country, by a specific service offering focusing on an industry, by region, or by function within a specific country. I use the term business unit for any of these entities that rely on the corporate office for guidance on formal communications.

Interviews

In writing this book, I interviewed a wide range of practitioners, both within the internal communications discipline and outside. I quote these experts throughout the book and identify the source for each quote in line. Appendix A, *Interviewee Biographies*, contains biographies for everyone who agreed to be identified. I also held interviews with several people who chose not to be named.

I quote repeatedly from two sources. The first is *Global Content Strategy: A Primer*[54] by Val Swisher. Swisher explains why you need a content strategy if you're operating globally, and she outlines the capabilities your tools and processes should have for managing content in multiple languages.

The second is Ed Catmull's *Creativity, Inc.*[10]. Catmull is one of the founders of Pixar Animation Studios, and the book is an inspiring how-to on managing creative teams. It's insightful, entertainingly written, and suitable for aspiring managers in any field. Now in its second edition, I can't recommend it enough.

Acknowledgements

I appreciate the time and insight of everyone interviewed, even if I wasn't able to name them here. Thanks to Dylan Tuttle, Lisa Raatz, and Jennifer Hahn, who read early drafts and gave me helpful feedback. Many thanks to the people of Content Wrangler and XML Press, who took what was to be an opinionated, self-published screed and helped me turn it into something I'm proud to call a book. And thanks to my dad, who never had an email address. Though he always asked about progress, I never thought to print out a draft. We always think we have more time.

The Landscape In Country

If it's true that English proficiency is a hiring requirement, why don't corporate communications get consumed overseas? Part I looks at realities from the perspective of local markets and explores some of the issues that they're either not telling you or that you're not hearing.

What You'll Learn: Who actually deploys communications in local settings, and what are the challenges they face in deploying deliverables from corporate headquarters.

Why You Should Care: The corporate headquarter's effort in global employee communications is largely wasted.

CHAPTER 1
The Challenges of Communicating Globally

When business people talk about corporate decision-making, they often use the battleship metaphor. They say this ship is so big that it can't change direction like a speedboat.

It's a cliché, but it's still a good metaphor. Even those of us who've never steered a battleship understand that building consensus in a big organization takes time.

Yet even the battleship, despite its size, can occasionally have an all-hands-on-deck meeting. That's not possible with global companies. If you need to coordinate action in multiple countries and in multiple languages, you need a better metaphor.

Running a global communications function is more like commanding a Mars rover. You're running the communication system at Mission Control. You're close to leadership and you understand the global strategy. But it takes hours for your instructions to reach the rover—something that not everyone in Mission Control seems aware of.

Once you dispatch an order, you and your team eagerly wait to hear the response. By the time an answer gets back to you on Earth, several more hours have passed and the rover is about to rotate out of range for another eight hours. Your engineers are gathered, impatient for the message. Did the corrective action work? If not, can you adjust? Do you have time to send a new set of instructions?

You receive the response, decode it, and read: "What did you say?"

Welcome to international communications.

Declaring English your corporate language is not a solution

Every global company I've worked with maintains that its corporate language is English—even if its headquarters are outside the US or the UK. They say that English is essential to people's daily work and that those who can't function in it are excluded during hiring. As a result, corporate departments assume that every message can be in English.

This is a fair assumption, especially in sectors like healthcare and technology, where staying on top of research and best practice requires English on a high level. Even in other fields, aspiring business people treat English as a basic job skill.

> Despite its ubiquity, declaring English the corporate language is self-serving.

However, unless you're in an English-speaking country, day-to-day interactions are almost always in another language. Establishing English as the standard puts corporate and regional relationships on an unequal footing. Imagine being asked to write just one email to a superior using your college Spanish. You'd feel a little nervous, and if you were asked to get your response out the same day, writing it might take all afternoon.

Worse, declaring English as your organization's official language enables complacency. It feeds the corporate delusion that *they* understand everything that *we* produce. People are naturally shy to speak up and ask questions, and internationally they're even more so. Fluency in English, after all, is one of the job requirements.

"We shouldn't think that English is English is English," said Leonard Rau, a senior brand strategist and Chicago-based Englishman. "It's not one language, because some live it while others learn it more formally. If you're born an English speaker, you have a different understanding than if you learn it as an adult. When I worked in Sweden, I found Swedes learn English correctly and adhere to the rules, but they have a hard time being creative with it. We natives are more inclined to play around."

People in the head office who speak their native language in every setting and channel have a clear advantage. But communicating exclusively in English has another significant side effect: it decreases the chances that a corporate communication will be read, since English content self-identifies as global and distant.

Most messages are forgettable

Carmen Simon is the founder of Memzy, a San Francisco-based company that uses neuroscience research to help businesses create and deliver memorable and actionable messages. She is the author of *Impossible to Ignore: Creating Memorable Content to Influence Decisions*[48]. She holds doctorates in both instructional technology and cognitive psychology and is an expert in presentation design, delivery, and audience engagement.

She says that messages in tune with a target audience's language and culture have a better chance of getting through. "To be on people's minds, you must become part of their reflexes, habits, and/or goals they consider valuable," she wrote[48].

In an interview, Carmen explained to me that a message inspires action only if people remember it, and that it's more memorable if it appeals to biologically innate reinforcers. She calls these primary reinforcers, and they are connected with our sensory memories. If a message can invoke the smell of grandma's kitchen, that message is more likely to be remembered and acted on.

She said that our primary reinforcers include the five senses, aesthetics, a sense of altruism, sex, and controlling one's environment. Since we call our first language our *mother* tongue, it's not hard to see that a message in that language connects more directly to these reinforcers.

As a rule, we don't communicate in the workplace about childhood or sex, so corporate messages have few of these primary reinforcers. Secondary reinforcers—rewards such as extra pay and promotions—are more plausible, but unfortunately, our day-to-day messages rarely have even these.

Simon writes, "The mistake some people make when trying to influence others' memory is that they overestimate the importance of goals and underestimate the impact of existing reflexes and habits"[48].

If we don't tap into their reflexes and habits, we appeal purely to intellect. Although we write about subjects important to employees, we aren't inspiring people to move toward them. And outside the Anglo-American world, we do this in a foreign language.

"Compared to reflexes and habits, communications in another language are things you have to think about," she told me. "You have to expend cognitive energy, which is in short supply. Cognition consumes twenty percent of the body's energy, which is why people fall asleep in presentations. Because we all get a certain amount of information through the day, we constantly want to preserve cognitive energy so that we can react in critical situations. We tend to prefer that which invites cognitive ease."[1]

Except for breaking news or mission critical messages, people postpone reading what's not in their native language, if they read it at all. We're all buried in email and content we mean to consume, but in the end, much of it slips by.

If some of your must-read queue is in a second language that you understand only with some effort, you will put it off. With time, the urgency passes and nothing bad happens. For audiences abroad, that cycle repeats, and they develop a detached attitude towards anything from the corporate office.

---

[1] For more on energy and cognition, see "Does Thinking Burn Calories? Here's What the Science Says"[22].

English-language read rates

I'm amazed by the high level of English proficiency in non-native speakers I work with, and it's important to recognize that lower read rates aren't just a matter of comprehension. You might expect low read rates in countries with lower English proficiency, but engagement with English-language content is lower even in countries such as the Netherlands and Sweden, where fluency in English is high. From specialists to managers to executives, people are more likely to read and act on content that's in their native language.

> No matter how proficient your audience is, announcements in English create a barrier to usability.

Jonathan Phillips, co-founder of Lithos Partners, a UK-based intranet consultancy, sees a limit to what English can do for a company. "You want employees to engage, to collaborate, and to communicate on a two-way basis. Providing a platform that's English-only will give you only an audience with fair competency in English. An English-only intranet will be limited to the US, the UK, and the main offices," he said. My experience bears those results out as well.

If you measure use of your internal channels, have a look for yourself. Everywhere outside the Anglo-American markets, English-only content lowers the read rate, click rate, and take-action rate. As a result, our beautifully executed work goes unopened, packed in crates, or in boldface in Outlook inboxes. Our work feeds cynical jokes about "another great idea from corporate."

We laugh at branding missteps,[2] but we can imagine how they happen— aggressive deadlines, limited budgets, and resource constraints are part of the story, but just as important, these missteps come from a failure to grasp that a few people at headquarters can't fully understand the interests of thousands of people worldwide.

---

[2] "20 Epic Fails in Global Branding"[25].

"Companies are finally waking up to fact that even in the best situations, if a culture doesn't want the same type of relationship with a brand that the company hopes for, audiences are going to laugh at branded content. In the worst case, they fall flat on their face with whoever they're courting and never recover," said Val Swisher in an interview.

The chances for cultural mistakes are just as great in employee communications, but when it comes to their own people, companies seem willing to come off as laughable. The risks are higher than they think.

> **Pitfall: The alienating English of the home office**
> What's interesting—and a little disheartening—is that language barriers only partially explain why corporate content doesn't get read.
>
> In settings where internal channels are measured, I've seen even less engagement with corporate, US-generated content among the English-speaking countries of the UK, Ireland, Australia, and New Zealand. Despite a shared language, these countries reject corporate messaging in sometimes even greater numbers. Those puzzling results tell us two things:
>
> - They understand but they see little value in corporate messaging
> - If content is important, it should be properly localized
>
> To get your ideas heard, you must make messages more relevant to local markets, rely less on global channels, and collaborate more with local resources to create more relevant and credible content.

Translation, localization, and co-creation

You have alternatives to creating one global version of content. Table 1.1 defines four approaches that may be familiar to people who create customer content, but less familiar to those in employee communications.

Table 1.1 – Four alternatives to English-only content

How it's done	Pro	Con
Re-creation		
Local staff decide what and when to translate without corporate knowledge or support.	It's already happening.	Higher risk of inaccuracy and low quality.
Translation		
Corporate translates content into target languages.	Professional communicators control the process, and it's faster than *localization* or co-creation.	The final product still sounds like corporate-speak.
Localization		
Corporate visually and verbally adapts a deliverable to local culture.	The content respects the audience and has a greater chance of getting noticed.	Localization takes more time, costs more, and adds complexity.
Co-creation or transcreation		
Trained local staff deliver relevant and unique content, key messages, and visual components.	Final content looks and feels local, relevant, and credible.	Co-creation and transcreation require investment, mutual trust, and local skills.

Employee engagement and the influence of communications

Marketers want customers to engage with their brands because they believe engagement builds an emotional connection that sustains relationships and drives sales. Companies want employee engagement for similar reasons.

Organizations with high levels of engagement provide better customer service, make better decisions[62], perform better in crises[58], have lower turnover, and are more profitable[5]. These studies, among others, show a strong link between engagement and many other positive outcomes. Likewise, low engagement contributes to a host of problems:

- Line-level management complains of low engagement when training doesn't stick or they have high turnover.
- Human resources says the company has low engagement because people don't take the annual survey or don't comply with corporate policies.
- Executives believe low engagement prevents people from recognizing and connecting with mission statements or the high-level strategies expressed in earnings announcements and corporate social responsibility reports.
- Corporate Communication departments see engagement as low when employees don't read content.

While each of these is true, improving the related content may not help. Human issues have the most influence on levels of engagement. Do I respect my boss? Do I have friends at work? Do I feel my work has purpose? These factors determine engagement far more than intranet content.

Engagement is hard to define and measure, but most agree that it's in short supply. Researchers tell us that worldwide, engagement in the workplace is at all-time lows[34], and at the time of writing, a Google search for "employee engagement crisis" yielded more than 22,000 results. If you have enthusiastic employees who devour your English corporate content, you're an exception. Employees pay more attention to local management than to corporate headquarters, so if they're engaged, it's despite your content, not because of it.

The myth of the information cascade

One concept in employee communications that many managers rely on is the cascade of information. Leaders share their ideas with management, sometimes with the help of Corporate Communications. Those managers are then responsible for passing the message down to lower-level managers and ultimately to line-level employees. The message is supposed to trickle down like water to everyone in the company. Many managers even use cascade as a verb (i.e., "Cascade this to everyone").

But information isn't water. A cascade that works well is tough to achieve, even in a company's home country. When cascading information to international employees, English creates an additional logjam. English-only messages block the flow not only for the psychological reinforcers that Simon outlined, but also for three predictable, organizational reasons.[3]

First, disseminating English content in some workplaces is forbidden by law. One communications director for a chemicals manufacturer with production plants in Europe, Asia, and Latin America assured me that they didn't have to bother translating internal content. Their personnel were highly educated and language wasn't a barrier.

> Local management determines when, how, and in what format your content is delivered.

I later met with the site director for one of their plants in Belgium, and I asked him how he used the communication content that he received from corporate. Looking slightly surprised, he said, "I don't share any of that."

He went on to say that for regulatory reasons written communication had to be in one of the local languages, so the only deliverables he shared with employees were locally created. Only managers ever saw corporate content.

---

[3] "When hierarchy meets the world of influence...or, "Why do we keep getting asked to do cascades when we know they don't work?""[27] explores the limits of cascades and hierarchical communications, and "The Negative Side of Cascading Information"[13] suggests there is a group-think dynamic in cascades, where people share information only when they want to associate themselves with the source. That may explain why managers who cascade information tend to do so without commentary or contextualization—something that Corporate Communications is desperately hoping for.

Intelligent and capable professionals—like the communications director for this chemicals manufacturer—routinely overlook the hard reality that their English-language deliverables can cause legal and labor problems if they're distributed beyond management, even if line-level employees are the intended audience.

Second, commercial differences can make corporate materials less useful. A company may be known as Company Inc. in the United States, but as Company GmbH in Germany. Seemingly small details like this can affect the logo and other design elements, and if the corporate materials don't match the local entity, they end up gathering dust.

Third, cascading across borders creates more work, leaving local business units responsible for *translation*, reformatting, and distribution. Unless the content is related to something local leaders want, or they feel compelled to put it out, they would rather (understandably) avoid the extra workload.

When the law requires a cascade

I argue throughout this book that you should localize and *co-create* content in partnership with local offices whenever possible. However, for public companies, localization is not advised for communications that are considered *material*. Material information refers to anything that could have an impact on the stock price. For example, when companies release their earnings, the results they report are material, and the content must be identical and simultaneously released in all markets.

While being drafted at corporate headquarters, material draft announcements are considered *privileged*, and they're tightly controlled until the moment they're released. The content is carefully reviewed by legal teams, and if it's translated, the documents are managed centrally. Once final, incongruities between translated versions and the global announcement could create legal problems. For material information, a cascade may be the best way to ensure compliance with disclosure requirements.

"Privileged communications apply to earnings, key staff changes, structure changes, anything that would be material information that the market needs to hear first," said Phillips. "It's a difficult business. But if you look at the scale of organizational communications, only a small percentage of output falls into that category. The rest has a degree of latitude."

How local businesses distort your message

Fluency is deceiving. With some English speakers, it's hard to believe that the language isn't native to them. Yet while you may forget there's a language barrier, they rarely do.

Local management is aware of such barriers, and if they think something is important, they translate it, with or without the involvement of the corporate office. Unless you've set up a localization system and have worked out who maintains and pays for it, the decision to translate is often ad hoc and by location.

Unknown to each other, several people in the same market may decide that something is important enough to be in the local language, so each one spends time recreating their own unique version. That's hardly an efficient use of resources, and it increases the chances of distorted and contradictory messaging.

> What you perceive as global deliverables may not appear in their original form.

Every deliverable from Communications appears in a wider context, and that context is usually uncoordinated and chaotic. Not only do local businesses create their own content, siloed global functions have local direct reports, and those functions simultaneously cascade content they deem important (e.g., training for IT, compliance, safety campaigns, etc.).

Like a Pachinko machine, corporate functions constantly dispense tiny balls of content that take unpredictable paths. Not only is the output from these various global functions uncoordinated, it can add up to a heavy local burden. In smaller markets it's likely that just one person is responsible for translations. Without optimization, those corporate functions may not realize the workload they've collectively put on that person.

Figure 1.1 – Pachinko parlor

The internal hodgepodge of the brand

A common way that local offices distort communications is in their use of visual brand elements. Many don't have access to the same tools as corporate content teams or to people who know how to use those tools.

People place higher value on content and documents that are branded and in the local language. But since local-language content is relatively rare, they may keep using translated content even after the brand elements are out of date. Or they re-create content as best they can with Microsoft Office, which is riskier in terms of brand compliance.

Few outside Communications understand or care about correct logo placement, font consistency, or tone. Every week, colleagues in the cubicles next to us at headquarters create ugly, outdated, and off-brand slides. Brand compliance in international locations can be even harder, where marketing and communications budgets are thin, resources skilled in those areas are few, and brand reviews are non-existent.

> **Practical Tip**
> If countries need to alter anything before distributing your deliverables, give them easy-to-use template versions of content, in standard tools such as Microsoft Office. For more on templates, see Chapter 10.

Mission and vision versus profit and loss

In global companies there's often tension between the corporate functions and local business units. "Corporate tends to focus on concepts like 'Our Purpose' and 'Our Mission,' while the business units have completely different priorities," said one senior communications strategy consultant in Chicago. "Local leaders want communications that talk about what drives their metrics, their bonus."

Business-unit metrics are typically based on profit, costs, and key performance indicators (KPIs) related to sales or service. Corporate may have global goals in areas like safety or sustainability, but unless they're part of local financial incentives, awareness of them can be low, let alone motivation to help achieve them.

Even for deliverables that are in demand—like case studies—it's difficult for corporate to get the necessary input without incentives. In-country leaders often don't see the urgency of requests from Corporate Communications because there's no tie-in to their KPIs. Many started in operations or sales, and they're rarely convinced that they need someone trained and fully dedicated to communications. "Local leadership feel that they're the ones who decide what's in the email, so why invest in a skilled person?" said the Chicago consultant.

With these entrenched beliefs, local leaders often assign someone from human resources or marketing, or an assistant to the chief executive, to execute communications. Even when you have that person's enthusiastic support, your goals in corporate communications are secondary to their main role. Their day job gives them plenty of other things to do, so even if they do what you ask (and some will not), the result is likely to be quickly thrown together to get it off their to-do list.

US content that thinks it's global

Not everything produced at headquarters is useful around the world. Some content is worthwhile from a US perspective, but it's not global. Be on the lookout for references like these that don't travel well.

Sports analogies

Some expressions are so common that it's easy to forget they came from sports. Hit it out of the park, a home run, punting on something, getting something past the goal line, March Madness, or the Super Bowl of _____(any competitive arena). Americans use such references so often that audiences abroad accept them with a shrug. Let's do better.

National Anything Day

"National Shout Out for Solar Day" may be a great event to mark in some places, but it's meaningless beyond US borders, and that includes Canada (hint: It's got national in the name). Instead, look out for international events, such as commemorative days promoted by the UN.

Holiday references

It should go without saying that the Fourth of July, Memorial Day, Labor Day, and Veterans' Day are celebrated only in the US. The same is true of Thanksgiving, Presidents' Day, and Groundhog Day. Unfortunately, I have to say it.

Shout outs

Common expressions may warm your voice and tone, but keeping up with current idioms is a struggle for non-natives. Create a plain-language version for international locations, and keep the popular expressions within your borders.

Pop culture references

I am always surprised at how much US celebrity news and reality TV shows are re-broadcast and covered abroad. Nevertheless, they're not for everyone. References to pop culture can come off as glib, cliquey, and condescending.

General culture references

Not all of us drive around the block to kill time or have lawns to mow. Best Buy gift cards aren't usable in every country, charities supported at the headquarters may not be known everywhere, and Girl Scout cookie deliveries and NCAA basketball tournament pools aren't global Even if everyone you know is talking about them, learn about these native references and cut them out of content. Let local communicators insert lifestyle references of their own.

Support of military personnel

Working with veterans is commendable. But other countries have a different relationship with the American armed forces, and US military bases in other countries aren't always admired. The US is in active conflict in several nations, and some of those conflicts are not supported by its allies. If your company works with veterans or active service members, that's great. But it's a local story.

Content with a sidebar of apology

Every country has its own references that are a mystery internationally. I speak English, but I have only a vague understanding of Boxing Day, *Coronation Street*, or the protocols of an audience with the Queen. You don't need to apologize for being American, you just need to recognize that the rest of the world exists. Apologies sound insincere if you repeat them each time you deliver content that is culturally specific to the home country.

CHAPTER 2
The Context for Local and Global Content

You aren't the only source for company content and news. You may be shouting from a commanding height, but employees hear more often from local colleagues, local management, and local staff in global functions such as IT, human resources, or marketing.

Figure 2.1 shows a typical range of content types that employees see. I've plotted them on two dimensions: global and local relevance.

Figure 2.1 – Local versus global relevance

The horizontal axis in Figure 2.1 shows the degree of local relevance. The further to the right, the more likely it is that content will be in the local language, be in formats that can be managed locally, and have references that resonate with daily reality.

The vertical axis shows the degree of global relevance. Content that is higher on this axis is more strategic and more relevant to greater numbers of business units. The higher on the global relevance axis a deliverable is, the more likely it was created at corporate. These messages align with global strategy and have a more long-term outlook. But they also tend to be abstract, in English, and lacking in local examples.

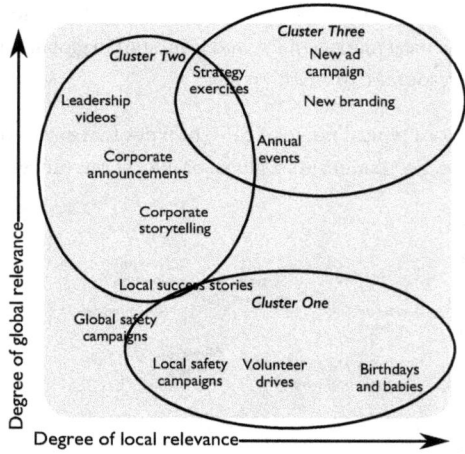

Figure 2.2 – Local versus global relevance: clusters

Although the details may vary, if you graph any organization's mix of local and corporate deliverables in this way, they will tend to form three clusters, each with its own strengths and weaknesses (see Figure 2.2).[1]

---

[1] Graphing your organization's mix of global and local content is a good exercise to evaluate opportunities and your readiness for localization and co-creation. For more preparatory steps, see Part II, "Leadership, Governance, and Budget."

Cluster one: locally generated content

Strengths

Communications near the horizontal axis are created and deployed within a country or on site. They're in the local language and people see them as coming from management and colleagues they know. These message can be safety campaigns, calls for community involvement, news of local hires, or photos from that day they had cake.

If you happened to be there, content about cake is highly relevant (which is why it's further to the right). But to people who weren't there, it's not interesting, which is why communicators like me cynically call this category *babies and birthdays*. Nevertheless, as much as I hate to admit it, this content gets viewed more than any other category. Babies-and-birthdays content is a natural part of working in a community, and while this kind of content has little strategic value, it's invaluable to the business.

Further to the left in cluster one is local content that's more business related. This content reflects specific business priorities and can include news of local results, volunteer drives, or safety campaigns.

Weaknesses

These communications have the advantage of being in the local language, but they often lack polish. Output that I see from local communications is often:

- Written to inform rather than persuade
- Visually unattractive, text only, or not compliant with brand standards
- Authoritative or nagging in tone
- Unconnected to company strategy

Some local content is better executed than that, but even when it looks good, it often misses larger opportunities. A piece of local content that congratulates a facility for achieving a certification may fail to mention

> Local communications are typically information-based and about as exciting as a phone directory.

where that certification fits into a larger strategy, what people had to do to achieve it, or what the company's long-term plans are for other facilities. Is this location leading the pack? Catching up? From the content as it's presented, it's impossible to tell.

Providing context connects an audience to something bigger, yet in my experience, local communicators focus on informing and almost always miss the chance to make that connection.

Local news, campaigns, and babies-and-birthdays announcements can be done better, but if challenged, local management often takes cover behind language and culture, saying that "Everyone here understands it." That may be true, but while Corporate Communications may be out of touch with local conditions, local businesses should learn to trust corporate's insight into best practices. Unappealing content and tone-deaf delivery have consequences, sending the unintended message that the company doesn't value its people.

Cluster two: corporate-generated content

Strengths

Content that headquarters creates has the most globalized outlook and applies to more people. This content includes leadership videos, town halls, news announcements, global campaigns, and more. In Figure 2.1, I graphed these communications on the left side near the vertical axis because they're typically produced in English. Announcements about big news events such as mergers or major advertising campaigns might be translated, but if they are it's a tightly controlled exercise coordinated with the legal department and centrally managed translation agencies.

Glocal and glocalization describe content and a process that have both global and local elements. This book aims to turn conventional global communications deliverables into something glocal.

Global deliverables are often created by more experienced professionals, using tools not available in Microsoft Office. They're fully approved, on message, timely, and in tune with the year's priorities. When they seek to persuade they often feature individual *recognition* and narratives. I call such content *corporate storytelling*. I've placed corporate storytelling further to the right because its real-life aspects can have more local relevance.

Weaknesses

Unique local conditions sometimes require unique local communications, but I question whether there is ever a case for global communications with no localization whatsoever. Just as the more cynical in the corporate communications department dismiss babies and birthdays, people in local business units are quick to judge global deliverables as vague platitudes direct from the Ivory Tower. Corporate Communications may see the Mission, Vision, and Values as three distinct text blocks, but others see them as one blob of abstraction.

Cluster two messages are in the voice of headquarters. Even when feature stories originate from local content, they're brushed up and re-purposed for worldwide consumption. Global content with real-life settings and examples have more credibility, which moves corporate storytelling slightly to the right. But this content is still rendered for universal appeal with little consideration for local perspectives. Even if a video's setting and employees are French, the tear-jerking music and testimonials drip English.

In Figure 2.1, I placed global and local safety campaigns near each other. In industrial settings, safety is a critical issue. Safety content gets produced by both global and local offices, but neither does it particularly well.

Global content on safety tends to arrive in the form of posters and videos of leaders talking generally about values (e.g., "Safety is Job #1"). Without specific references to local work practices, English deliverables like these are hopelessly abstract. Local leadership hardly improves them. They often replicate these messages in the local language but imitate global content, leaving it equally abstract. The visuals can be crude and the tone can be scolding condescension.

The problem with this kind of content is that no one needs to be *informed* of the need for safety; they need to be *persuaded* that it's important. No one slices their hand open because they were unaware that it would be a bad idea; they slice their hand open because they felt time pressure and ignored protocols. I look again at this important but problematic area of communications in Chapter 16, *Working with Your Network*.

Cluster three: global/local hybrid content

The upper right-hand corner of Figure 2.1 shows initiatives where corporate works with local countries to translate, shape, and deliver content. The subjects are often predictable events such as annual celebrations, leadership meetings, or coverage of annual goals and performance.

I placed brand-related events here too. These events occur less frequently, but they're accompanied by more fanfare. They typically have funding and planning for local-language versions, especially if corporate needs local organizations to take action.

Content localized by regions or countries—such as providing context about a change in sales strategy or service delivery—would be further to the right.

Strengths

This kind of content gets far more views than the other two, probably because when people buy in they promote content more earnestly. Because of the annual cadence or the perceived value, local staff are often ready to help with translation and distribution.

In projects related to brand initiatives and advertising, production timelines are usually longer, and it's easier to find people willing to participate. Employees seem to find such campaigns more interesting, corporate is more willing to pay for translations, and local management is more willing to pay attention to precise wording for tag lines and messaging.

For annual campaigns, local staff may have been involved before, know that it's coming, and understand how it will benefit their profit center. In my experience, making time for even a little local shaping gives initiatives more internal buzz. Maybe it's because they're new, colorful, and in the local language, but these moments get more notice mostly because local and global staff are working together. We need more of this.

Weaknesses

Because of its complexity, this kind of content is rare. If there's no formal system in place, the project cobbles together resources and processes, which lengthens the timeline and can negatively affect quality. If the people involved don't communicate/localize regularly, misunderstandings and delays in the project timeline are common. Because it's a special project, those involved have to balance their participation with everyday tasks, which is a hidden cost to the organization.

Graphing your employee deliverables

If your company is global, each piece of content for employees usually falls into one of the three clusters shown in this graph.

- Cluster one: in local language but often not in compliance with corporate standards and unrelated to company strategy
- Cluster two: better looking, globally focused, abstract, and in English
- Cluster three: some kind of hybrid, with a broad range of execution quality depending on local capabilities

In my experience, almost all day-to-day communications are either cluster one or cluster two. Cluster three, *glocal* hybrids are prepared only on special occasions.

Every company has its own spectrum of local and global communications. Maybe you have good localization for subtitled leadership videos or you've created workable templates for routine IT announcements. Ideally, the majority of communications that employees see would be in cluster three: in local language, high quality, device neutral, timely, and with enough local detail to resonate with the target audience.

If your company manages to produce only a few deliverables in cluster three, or if the quality of those deliverables varies, it may be due to inflexible corporate materials or inadequate local skill sets.

This book is about finding ways to produce more deliverables in cluster three. You may not be able to achieve co-creation in all of your markets, but you can get much closer than you are today with a little planning, even without huge budgets.

Measuring international communications

Measuring communications has always been tricky, but if you expect to communicate globally, you have to understand what's happening. And yet it continues to surprise me how few organizations measure readership of internal content.

If they took time to look, they'd probably see few people outside the home country engaging with internal content. In fact, global readership is normally so low that it makes me wonder what cost-conscious executives would do if they were aware of it.

Instead, unmeasured content perpetuates the status quo. Communications departments blindly assume that almost everyone watches the CEO's videos, and corporate managers demand exposure in global channels because they assume wide readership.

Many of the demands placed on corporate communication departments are to complete tasks that experience tells them are ineffective (for example, launching a newsletter). Without data, there's no way to push back on these demands. If you can show that global deliverables have little impact outside the home country, you can better argue against the reactive tactics that burden most internal communication departments.

International audiences bring complexity, but the unique conditions in which local business units operate create opportunities to experiment, pilot, and compare results. With data, you can identify effective tactics and focus your energy on them.

Collecting quantitative data: local considerations

Like all of us, communication departments are susceptible to the dopamine release of page views, likes, comments, and shares. Unfortunately, we don't get much of that from international employees. Moreover, international employee demographics make many digital content measures less meaningful.

Few multinational organizations offer the same services or have the same level of brand recognition across all of their markets. Yet few in corporate seem aware that different countries have different operating models, sell different products, and target different customers.

Here are some local conditions that can have an impact on international measurement and analysis of digital content:

- **Different demographics:** A company might have a unique business model to serve one country, or that country's largest product or service might be just a minor offering back home, or perhaps the country outsources a function that headquarters thinks of as core to the business. Differences like these can give a local market an entirely different mix of employees.

  For example, higher readership of content in France may seem like a bit of good news, but if you looked at their business model, you'd see that blue-collar operations are outsourced and that employees there are computer-based office workers. Unless you're comparing their readership to other office workers, the measure is invalid.

- **The local and global news mix:** In larger, more mature offices, local staff probably create their own content, so a lead story from corporate headquarters may get buried below the fold. In smaller countries, the operation may be more like a startup with a few people in one office, and elaborate digital campaigns may feel like overkill when they can talk with their colleagues face to face. Since each office selects which of your materials to use, the overall context for communication deliverables is different.

- **Platforms not connected:** You may not be using the same communication platform. I've seen internal firewalls that hinder access to channels in some countries, especially if they joined the company through a merger or acquisition. Privacy regulations or licensing issues may keep some countries out, and while SMS text notifications may be used in the home market, it's unlikely they're sent beyond that. Audit your channels and know precisely where functionality such as send to all is—or isn't—available.

Collecting qualitative data: avoiding distortion

Getting attention and inspiring action in the field has always been difficult, in English or any language. For corporate, useful feedback is hard to come by and that's especially true internationally. If something wasn't received well (or not at all), local businesses won't volunteer that information.

Unless they're empowered and motivated, it's likely that business units aren't localizing global initiatives at all. When they choose to deploy corporate's work, they often follow instructions to the letter, distributing it with no changes.

Afterward, they notify Corporate Communications that the program was launched. Feedback is minimal, and the creators wonder what they did wrong. When the corporate office insists on feedback, they'll answer with what they think the head office wants to hear.

Maybe they're being considerate of the campaign creator's feelings, but they know that if they tell the truth, the second question will be about what went wrong. Since they were the messengers, they're hesitant to report an outcome that might lead to them being asked to do it over, or run a focus group to find out why the campaign failed.

Figure 2.3 – Global campaign launches don't always go according to plan

Local communicators don't always understand that corporate relies on them to translate its ideas, not just its content, and it frustrates them that their local partners don't already see this.

Local staff don't want to conduct postmortems over corporate projects. They want to get back to work.

Both sides are failing in their responsibilities. Corporate Communications is overconfident in its ability to craft meaningful content, and local business units are passive, expecting ready-made content they can deploy without additional effort.

Corporate Communications must recognize—and convey to local markets—that they can't design and fine-tune a campaign so perfectly that it will arrive suitable for immediate deployment in every location. Corporate must also understand that the messaging, toolkits, and content that they provide will be executed by people with different goals and different levels of experience than the communicators in the home office. Local businesses select what they think they need from corporate content, then deliver it using whatever tools they have. Unless corporate effectively communicates about its purpose with them in advance, the local business will likely miss strategic elements.

> **Practical Tip**
> Before communicating an initiative, discuss the costs and benefits of translating content with local teams. Work with them to determine how to communicate your message in a way that benefits the business.

Technology barriers to internal communication

Companies strive for consistency and uniformity, but in practice the technologies people use probably vary. You may see employees in your office using the same model laptop, but assume nothing.

Business units that were brought together through a merger or acquisition may be working with legacy technology or devices, especially in smaller countries. There may be privacy laws that restrict measurement of email. In countries like Germany, introducing social media channels to reach employees requires consent of *works councils* (legally required committees of employee representatives), and that approval can drag on for months.

Your intranet may be biased toward desktops—and therefore office employees—which can leave out large parts of the organization. John Yunker, cofounder of Byte Level Research and author of *Think Outside the Country*[63], writes that in many parts of the world, internet access is entirely through mobile devices. "More than 120 million Chinese experience the internet through their smartphones and only their phones"[63].

Technology solutions to address these complicated scenarios are always evolving, so I won't recommend specific tools. But don't dismiss these barriers as outlying situations that affect only small user groups. When it comes to user experience across borders, assume your tools have nothing in common until you verify otherwise. Recognize where access is lacking and develop strategies to deal with it alongside the local business.

User experience is unlikely to be the same around the world. Until you audit technical capabilities in your communication systems, beware of calls-to-action that overpromise. Content that you think is "in the palm of their hands" or "at the tips of their fingers" may not be accessible everywhere. Such unrealistic promises frustrate employees and confirm their suspicion that corporate is out of touch with work-day realities.

Reaching the non-employee workforce

There are people who deliver your company's services, who work on premise, who wear a uniform, and who serve as the face of the company.

And yet you can't talk to them.

That's because in some markets your company contracts third parties to complete the work. Outsourcing is a common practice for global companies operating in Western Europe, due to the region's labor costs and protections that make it more difficult for employers to lay off workers. They also outsource in countries like China that restrict foreign business activity.

Since these workers aren't employees, there can be legal limits on how and when you're allowed to communicate with them. Your human resources and legal departments will likely advise you that inviting contractors to company-wide events is off limits, as is including contractors in all-employee emails. Even a poster can be problematic. In facilities where contractors work alongside employees, a poster with the company's logo can imply that anyone in that workspace is an employee.

If contractors can convince a court that they're being treated as de facto employees, the company may have to pay fines, compensate them with back pay, or give them long-term contracts and employee benefits.

These limits make it especially tricky to communicate across regions or globally. While preparing for a company-wide event, you might discover that it can't be held in some facilities because they're staffed wholly or in part by contractors. You may find that you can't require contractors to take an online training, or that if you can, they don't have access to your web training platform. When local management informs the corporate office about such issues, they get shrugged off as local details that the regions need to deal with.

That's an abdication of duty. Communications in the age of outsourcing is more complex than ever, and the regions and countries probably don't have legal staff on premise to help them sort it out. In abdicating, the corporate office leaves the company vulnerable to labor disputes and communication breakdowns during crises. As frustrating and complex as this issue is, the communications department must come to grips with the labor mix and plan for it.

Whether your company uses franchise partners, preferred vendors, contractors, or contingent workers, the conditions will vary from country to country. To understand current practice and what's allowed, work with the functions in your company that have a stake in the issue. That could include legal, labor, human resources, operations, and communications.

> It's not impossible to reach contractors, but you must be cautious.

These stakeholders will give you a more complete picture, but in most markets, Corporate Communications should never attempt to communicate directly to external resources. Line-level managers are allowed to give contractors instructions related to routine work or in response to an emergency, but for much of the workplace's mass communication, if you want to reach contractors, you have to go through their employer, who will select the content they want to share. You can suggest that they convey a specific message, but you can't order them to.

It's not impossible to reach contractors, but you must be cautious. Topics such as how to speak about the brand with customers, operational procedures, equipment instructions, and compliance with policies on anti-corruption may be allowable only during on-boarding.[2]

Even content that the corporate office is confident will help people sell more or keep them safe must be framed not as orders, but as best practices that your company recommends rather than demands. Some legal and human resource departments may forbid even these. Nevertheless, once the corporate office understands the client/contractor relationship, there may be ways to get non-emergency, motivational, and educational content to them.

Corporate Communications should have a practical understanding of how to reach external contractors, legally and on time. You need to audit your target audience, learn who's external, find out how best to reach them, what limits must be respected, what channels are available, and of course, what the contractor audience is interested in hearing.

Just as with your own internal communications practices, you need to look at systems, people, and incentives. The issue of outsourcing is among the myriad reasons that you need *in-country review* of deliverables, and maybe even a site-by-site review. I look more at the in-country reviews in Chapter 8, *Preparing for Localization*.

The issue of communicating with contractors isn't going away. Even if your company isn't doing business this way today, it may merge with or acquire one that does. The need to communicate with contractors can come up at any time, so it's best to get ready now.

---

[2] In an era of social responsibility reporting, this issue is especially tricky. Your company wants to assure the marketplace that all of its operations and partners are on board with its anti-bribery and anti-corruption policies, yet these practices can be reinforced only through the initial work contract (i.e., If you're caught doing this, we'll stop doing business with you). You may remind employees routinely of their responsibilities, but such reminders to contractor employees is beyond your reach.

When you audit the processes of communicating with contractors, here are some questions to ask human resources and other stakeholders:

- In which markets/countries are we deploying contractors?
- Who owns or oversees that commercial relationship?
- What functions are the contractors performing?
- Do they work in our facilities?
- Are there any legally mandated local requirements regarding communications?
- How does our company communicate with these contractors today?
- If we had to make a procedural change today, how would we communicate this change to contractors?
- Which facilities or functions are exclusively staffed with contractors, and which ones are staffed with a mix of contractors and employees? Which ones have only our employees?
- Do the contractors use our equipment?
- Does their equipment or tools display our brand?
- Do these contractors interact with customers? With employees? Under what circumstances?

CHAPTER 3
Translation Challenges

If its campaigns are translated at all, the corporate office allows little time for it, thinking translation is a simple, short task. It isn't. This chapter looks at complications that make some global managers' expectations unrealistic.

Corporate functions commonly plan in isolation. They think once their content is approved at headquarters, international distribution follows immediately after. Managers in areas like compliance or product development who aren't familiar with global projects often don't know they need to budget time for translation or how to prepare for it.

Even when translation is factored into a project, managers think it's a nearly automated process, where an English original is submitted and other language versions appear magically the next day. If you've ever worked with translations, you know that behind the scenes, translators struggle with badly written originals and jargon they don't recognize.

Originals and translations are not identical

Learning a language is something I didn't try until I had to. My bachelor's degree required two years of language study, and I naively chose Russian. I didn't know any Russian speakers, so my concept of the language was remote and abstract. Even after two years of quizzes and exams, I thought translation was a one-to-one, word-for-word exchange that was worked out like a formula. You look up each word in the dictionary and assemble a translation. You look up apple and there you have it. On to the next word.

I hear people mistakenly thinking the same way, and this misperception prevents them from understanding the problems of language difference and machine translation. They think getting a few hundred words translated should take a couple of hours and that the final document will be equivalent. Multilingual people know that it's more complicated than that.

Years later I moved to the Czech Republic and began learning Czech. Living in that country and struggling to make myself understood gave me a different understanding of the challenges. I quickly learned the word *apple* was one thing, but expressions like "How do you like them apples?" was something else entirely. A word-for-word translation just wouldn't make sense.

For some words, there isn't an equivalent. We borrow words like zeitgeist because there isn't a match in English. In business conversations in other languages, you hear English words like email, Six Sigma, and other expressions that speakers can't translate.

There is also the issue of style. Translators are writers, and some write better than others. I once picked up a novel translated from a German author I'd never heard of. I liked it so much I bought another by the same writer and the same publisher. The first was beautiful and mysterious. The second was dense and unreadable. The publisher had used different translators, and the results were completely different.

> Translation is an art. Different artists make different creative choices to render content that retains—in their view—as much of the tone and intention of the original.

In corporate contexts, a translator's choices can be based on a variety of factors, including the urgency of the deadline, the translator's personal preference, their understanding of the industry or organization, their values, and more. The choices translators make can be beautifully simple or awkward and ambiguous.

> Even if you don't speak another language, grasping the limits of translation will help you make better decisions about when to translate, and help you understand what kind of results to expect.

"If you think translation is just a matter of word for word, rent a foreign movie," said one translation manager at a US-based multinational. "Subtitles can be really out there."

The problem of bad business writing

Bad professional writing is a barrier to all kinds of communication, and there's no quick fix.

Required reading in my college composition classes was Strunk and White's *The Elements of Style*[49] and George Orwell's essay "Politics and the English Language"[40]. Orwell connected pretentious jargon and other bad writing with civic responsibility. Both took examples of bloated academic and bureaucratic writing and showed how to fix them. Both stressed that writers must respect readers and work toward clear, accessible writing.

The rush and volume of email has made things worse, and bad writing bogs organizations down. An unclear email message sent to all employees has costs. Even if only seventy percent of employees open the message, it's still a huge waste of time if they don't understand it.

Content from IT is notoriously unclear, and not just because the topic is specialized. It's because their writing is usually incompetent. Bad writing affects sales. Do proposals and presentations distinguish your company, or do they just re-arrange the same buzzwords competitors use?

Orwell and Strunk and White are right even today, and new books still get written about clear writing. The style all these manuals favor is at the core of the plain-language movement. The Plain Language Association International[1] wants people to understand the value of clear expression in any language, which they define this way: "A communication is in plain language if its wording, structure, and design are so clear that the intended audience can easily find what they need, understand what they find, and use that information."

---

[1] https://plainlanguagenetwork.org/plain-language/what-is-plain-language/

Naturally I'm convinced that bad writing is a problem: I've been editing and compiling badly written input into content for years. But I'm not alone.

- Val Swisher, CEO of Content Rules, writes, "Lots of wasted time equals lots of wasted money. And wasted time can also mean delays, which cost even more money. In addition, because long sentences have to be interpreted and reinterpreted, it is possible that each translation has a different meaning"[54]. Swisher also cites bad writing in a LinkedIn article: "Three (Surprising) Reasons for Poor Quality Translations"[55].
- When I asked Mark Ohlsen, CEO of LRS Recording in Chicago, how to keep costs down when localizing video, the first thing he said was, "Make sure that your script is well written. Mistakes are going to be reflected in the translation."
- Josh Bernoff, author of *Writing Without Bullshit*[6], regularly blogs about bad writing. His *Daily Beast* article, "Bad Writing Costs Businesses Billions"[7], talks about how much unclear writing can cost businesses.

Cost-conscious companies should pay more attention to the quality of their source content. First drafts are typically a jumble of thoughts, and simplifying takes time. Unfortunately, in a highly technical and time-constrained world, people don't complete that step. As a result, corporate functions continue to churn out bad English that arrogantly passes as universal.

Governments and companies are concerned about a skills gap in science, technology, engineering, and mathematics (STEM fields),[2] but they don't pay the same attention to writing. Complex business-speak is so widespread that content from any department could use editing and quality reviews.

Fortunately, some companies are being forced to use plain language in disclosures and customer agreements. Deborah S. Bosley of The Plain Language Group says that when they do, her clients discover additional cost benefits.

"Companies come to me for two reasons," she said. "The first is the force of regulation. The financial industry is increasingly required to disclose

---

[2] "The Evolution of the Skills Gap Requires 21st Century Solutions"[38].

information in plain language. The second is because they're getting complaints from customers. That adds costs to call centers or maybe contributes to losing customers. More and more companies recognize that plain language is good business."

Bad business writing also makes it harder to go global. If your original content is dense, your translations will be less accurate and more expensive. According to Transcend,[3] a language services company in Davis, California, "Plain language documents are typically 40% shorter than the original, and printing, paper, and translations costs are lowered because there are fewer words and fewer pages."

In-country reviews with adequate timelines are a good first step to mitigating some of the drains on productivity caused by difficult, unclear English content.

The true costs of translating content internally

Headquarters generally don't set aside budget for translation of internal content, and they leave it to local markets to decide. Local countries don't want to spend money on it either, so they hand off the task to someone in the office. Some companies report that they've successfully crowdsourced translations among employees. Free solutions like these may seem appealing if you have no budget for translation, but they overlook the real costs.

You might imagine it a friendly request, but you're asking a bigger favor than you realize. Busy people tend to do favors for strangers in a hurry. They're not going to be as concerned about quality or global brand standards, and if it's a big campaign that comes to them as a surprise, as many of these requests do, it may even spark resentment.

> Even if you're not paying a vendor, there's no such thing as free translation.

Second, it doesn't matter how proficient they are in English. It's a misperception that any bilingual person can translate. Trained professionals do

---

[3] https://transcend.net/services/PL.html

it faster and more accurately, and unless someone with credentials as a translator gets assigned to do the job, quality will suffer.

Holiday content is something that's especially likely to be insourced. One example was a branded, multi-lingual holiday greeting card, probably created using Google Translate. The main image was a tag-cloud arrangement of "Happy Holidays" in several languages. The translation came up with well-meaning, but never used, neologisms. (The Czech and Polish back-translated to "good vacation," a nonsense phrase). For a company that claims to be diverse and globally aware, that's embarrassing.

In another holiday example, human resources prepared employee gift boxes with "Merry Christmas" in each language of the region printed on the surface. They tapped *native speakers* in the region office to translate and review the proofs. When the boxes were distributed, a few Dutch employees pointed out a typo. Human resources had completed the project with internal resources and at minimal cost, but the end result gave Dutch readers the impression that the language wasn't important enough to warrant an additional review.

Internal communications is continually trying to get by with limited budgets, so it's likely we'll keep approaching our employees to help us translate. But if we continue to depend on these internal, good-faith resources to adapt and execute our communications, we should be prepared to accept misunderstandings, misinterpretations, resistance, and delays.

For every global deliverable, the costs and benefits of translation should be assessed financially, logistically, and politically. It's important to grasp that whether there's an invoice or not, translations have real costs, and we shouldn't just demand it like we're shouting an order into a drive-through microphone.

Getting what you pay for: translation is not a commodity
Companies struggling with translation have root problems extending wider than corporate communications. For global entities, translation is an issue across the company, and left to their own devices, departments and business units come up with their own solutions. As a result, companies end up with

multiple translation vendors and eventually, the procurement department takes notice. The number of vendors, the total company spend, and the commoditized prices of the language services industry make translation a natural target for optimizing and streamlining.

I interviewed one internal communications manager whose company was at that stage. They had just begun to appreciate their translation complexities, and he was tasked with benchmarking their practices, selecting a single worldwide vendor, and developing a unified process.

Along the way, he looked at a dozen global companies in various industries. Of those benchmarked, he concluded that technology companies had the most advanced practices, thanks to many years of managing high volumes of documentation for global releases.

Despite those differences in maturity, he said that global companies often struggle with issues that are similar. One is the creation of an accurate glossary of unique or proprietary terms. Even though they're used over and over internally, they get rendered by different translators in different ways, leading to inconsistency, confusion, and even breakdown. "We may be talking about a specific lever in a specific tractor, and that's a word that needs to be translated correctly 100% of the time. An incorrect translation might not just dilute your brand, it could kill somebody. A consistent glossary is critical."

A second issue is ongoing price pressure. "You can't treat translation like you're buying paper clips. Procurement may know the per-word rate for a specific language, but if that's all they're looking at, you create a bunch of other problems," he said. "Companies that look only at price are typically at the beginning stages of their localization program."

He adds that since translation services are a competitive market, providers are always pitching to local business units. Even if your company has a global vendor, if translation costs are allocated to local balance sheets, business units may find these pitches attractive.

"Various parts of an organization may be tempted down that path of choosing a commoditized solution for an immediate problem. When they do that, they lose opportunities to manage costs and any possibility of managing the glossary," he said. "It also results in duplicate effort. There's time spent with administration, people managing the process for the first time, inputting new vendors into the system and so on. Project management time ends up being days instead of a few hours."

I look at ways to improve translation practices in Chapter 9.

CHAPTER 4
Visual Communication

People want attractive visuals. My career focus has been mostly in writing, but in employee communications, people don't come to my team because they want something written well. They come because they want something to look good.

When people think of my function's output, they picture the work of a designer. I envy designers their cool factor, but they deserve it. Strong visuals help get ideas across to more people, including skimmers, non-native speakers, and even writers like me. They play a huge role in making concepts clearer to international audiences.

But it's a mistake to assume that visuals always work the same everywhere. How people interpret photos, graphics, and colors is influenced by culture, and even high-quality images can have low impact or even cause problems in the wrong context.

Despite the value of good visual design, most organizations find it too expensive to keep skilled resources in-house, which limits their ability to create and manage culturally appropriate visuals. This chapter outlines some of the difficulties with executing visuals internationally.

> **Practical Tip**
> It's not possible for any one of us to know everything that will resonate with or offend an audience. Use your organization's desire for good-looking visual content as an argument in favor of better localization and co-creation. Even cost-conscious leaders will occasionally spend on content that's visually impressive.

Limitations of visual communication

> "The tools for creating rich visual content keep getting better and better … The bar is coming down for how difficult or easy it is to make visual content. That's great, and yet there are a lot of technical content teams that still have to battle for time and resources to really create and maintain visuals. Some teams have gone so far as to strip out all visuals and just have this wall of text."
> —Daniel Foster, Content Wrangler webinar[20]

Employee communications can also be limited by inflexibility and unavailability of visual assets. Thanks to online templates and creative apps, people can easily make attractive announcements for class reunions and family holiday letters, but internal corporate departments struggle to maintain brand standards, update content with new visuals, and maintain a collection of images they can legally use.

As with marketing content, simply eliminating visuals is not an effective way to deal with these complications. In his webinar, Foster looks at research that shows why you can't afford to produce content without visuals.

Managing photography

Creating and managing legally usable images in a central repository—also referred to as a *digital asset management system* or DAM—is a common practice. If implemented well, a DAM reduces costs, saves time for business units, and mitigates the risk of unauthorized use.

At its best, a DAM provides ways to catalog images using tags and *metadata* so that assets can be easily located by content creators. A good DAM makes it easy to use images no matter what publishing tool or channel you use.

Having curated images available can be especially useful to local business units that are busy with their own responsibilities. But it's also typical for employees to complain that they can't find anything they want to use in the image repository managed by corporate.

That's because those repositories are typically not really DAMs, and keeping a repository up to date isn't easy. What companies often have instead is an image bank as part of their intranet's *Content Management System (CMS)*. They may call it a DAM, but unless the image bank is also accessible to other content publishing tools, it's just one of probably many repositories.

Corporate repositories may include images acquired in the past, and commercial rights to those images may not last forever. Even in-house images expire. Employees in a photo may no longer be with the company or they may never have given permission to use it. Tracking usage rights is complex, and keeping the library stocked can be both time consuming and expensive.

In an interview, Alan J. Porter, author of *The Content Pool*[70], described an issue that many face with images. "Many companies don't have a DAM, and internal content is sitting on SharePoint or on laptops. They've got content but they can't find it. As a result, they re-create over and over again. Or people go to Google Images, which leaves them vulnerable to issues over usage rights. Or they buy rights to the same image over and over without realizing it. Unless they've got a DAM and they're putting together metadata and taxonomies around images so that people can find them, nobody knows what they've already got."

With conventional tools, most of us lack the time, imagination, or skills to comply with *brand guidelines* for images and photos. So we either repeatedly use the same small set of photos or go off brand and hope not to get caught. Expanding the pool of available images helps people all over the company, and some CMS systems include an image subscription service, giving users unlimited access to photos, images, and video.

In international settings, the usable bank of images is typically small. Corporate images are usually limited to those sourced in the home country, and the curators of those images often have cultural bias. Val Swisher illustrated this with a mailbox to show how images are cultural in *Global Content Strategy: A Primer*[54]. An icon of a blue mailbox seems natural in the US, but in other countries, mailboxes are different colors and shapes. People choosing images for global use may not be aware of those differences, and their selections can limit the number of images that are effective in other countries.

Moreover, photos are not interpreted the same everywhere. Browse available collections of photos in business settings, and you'll mostly see startup meetings in coffee shops or staged groups delighted about something on a laptop. They feel about as authentic as models in a clothing catalog, and people sense an American value system in the depiction. Even in-house photos aren't universal. Background details often give away the location, letting viewers know that it's a corporate stock photo, not local.

Leonard Rau has worked in brand strategy across Europe and the US, and he says that photos seen as diverse and positive in the US are rejected elsewhere as naïve American stereotyping. "The perfect global image just doesn't exist," he said. "We don't live in a monoculture. A picture of US dollar bills to represent money is so ambiguous. A hackneyed photo of a racially diverse business team doesn't work universally. I wish we would stop trying to squeeze that square peg into a round hole."

Moving away from a reliance on photography might be a useful tactic. Porter told me about one client, a multinational heavy engineering company, that began examining a new DAM to serve its customer website. They decided to replace photos of their products, which showed them in use in specific climates, with drawings that were independent of setting. They quickly found more than a dozen different internal use cases for the drawings. Because they implemented a DAM and correctly categorized the images, they were available to other groups. Companies in any industry can benefit from a system that makes legally usable images findable to all business units, especially images that are culturally neutral.

Managing graphics

When companies opt to use graphics, keeping design and layout in the hands of professionals can make international versions easier to manage. The business units responsible for adapting graphics rarely have the budget to purchase graphic design tools and often lack experience in putting them to use. As a result, companies often centrally create a small number of graphical designs to use with translated content.

"People in the field are distant. You'd have to have tight feedback loops built into the process, which isn't easy. There are only so many times I can tell someone who isn't a designer to swap a color or move something a couple of pixels. It's cheaper and easier to do it myself," said Arlene Birt, Chief Visual Storyteller for Minneapolis-based Background Stories, an information design consultancy specializing in transforming concepts related to sustainability into visual stories.

Execution may be easier to manage with central creation, yet smaller language groups are often neglected because corporate doesn't create versions for all of the company's languages. Even for local business units that are fortunate to be provided with translations, they may see the look and feel as something alien and corporate. That lowers the chance of holding attention and resonating locally.

Managing video

Using video in multiple markets has challenges that limit quality and increase costs. Management often wants videos for employees, thinking it's just a matter of creating and posting. It's an easy misunderstanding. There's so much video on social media that people think that making it happen must be easy. But in commercial settings, it never is.

Talking-head videos

Video is consumed more often than text,[1] but if it's only in spoken English, the audience worldwide could be limited. The reach can be expanded with localization, but it's easy to overlook the costs. Even for a simple talking-head leadership video, costs grow quickly with each additional language. If you want to go for more regional or global reach, your first decision is whether to dub or subtitle it.

---

[1] "11 Reasons Why Video is Better Than Any Other Medium"[12].

People in small language groups see less dubbing and are more used to subtitles. Smaller countries' commercial media have limited buying power, so running Anglo-American content in its original language is common in places such as the Netherlands and Scandinavian countries. Larger countries such as Germany and Italy can afford dubbed versions. These market realities can shape preferences for dubbing. The users you're targeting can also be important. People with less English proficiency might prefer dubbing, and those who are driving may need to listen instead of read.

However, adding subtitles seems to be the most useful way to localize. Even in markets that expect dubbing in movies, many prefer hearing the actual voice of their company's leaders. With streaming media and amateur YouTube tutorials, original language video is consumed more and more.

Subtitles help get the message across in other settings too. Video used in work environments such as break rooms will probably be displayed without sound. An endless loop with audio in a closed space quickly becomes annoying. For my own social media consumption, I prefer a video to have subtitles so that I can view it silently, and I'm more likely to skip videos that don't have them.

Globalizing a leadership video may pose additional obstacles beyond the question of whether to dub or use subtitles. Mark Ohlsen is the founder and CEO of Chicago-based LRS Recording, a provider of foreign-language localization services for multimedia. His book *Insider's Guide To The Foreign Language Video Marketplace*[37] lists six derailments that can prevent a video's global distribution. If you spot any of these in your script, skip the translation and let the English version do what it can.

- **Narration speed:** If the speaker talks quickly, especially about lofty, abstract topics like earnings, it will be hard to capture details in the space available for subtitles.
- **Quick video cuts:** When the scene changes frequently, it gives the narrator/subtitling less time to get the point across.
- **Source content readability, style, and consistency:** Folksy humor or jargon can take more time to explain in other languages, and bad writing may not translate well.

- **English-language humor:** Charismatic leaders may be used to working the crowd, but jokes rarely translate well and may even offend.
- **English-language slang:** Some concepts are cultural or take more space to explain than the video frame allows.
- **Acronyms:** A few internal acronyms are global, but many others are not. If a video uses an acronym as a mnemonic device, it won't be memorable to non-English-speaking audiences.

Leaders and communications professionals frequently overlook these derailments. When considering a video for international use, Ohlsen advises that a video localizer look at the script first to check for things that are either untranslatable or that drive up production costs.

Crowd-sourced, employee-produced videos

"Just have someone shoot it on their phone," said every executive eager to get a campaign started.

Social media and sophisticated tools have deluded us into thinking it's easy to create good video. Crowd-sourced videos that celebrate a sense of global community sound like a good idea, but low international participation says otherwise.

Ohlsen says successful crowd-sourced video is the exception. "It can work. You see people going live on Facebook all the time, and a lot of people can put a story together succinctly and it works. But I work with more than 140 media production companies, and when they have to deal with amateur video from phones, they're all crying. Everybody's phone is different, and then you're slogging through hours of footage trying to find a diamond."

Cleaning up video and audio can be time consuming, and those hours come at a cost. You can attempt it in house, but inexperienced people editing video can be a huge time commitment, and you still may not get great footage. While our Facebook friends may be willing to watch amateur video, attracting strangers to video is something else. Lighting, screen orientation, and especially audio can all contribute to low-grade video that users reject.

Another drag on a global call for local video is confidence in English. I've seen clients frustrated when they ask employees overseas to create first-person video and get no response, even when those requests should be easy to fulfill. There may be multiple reasons for that, but first among them has to be shyness. Many of us don't like seeing ourselves in video, and outside the Anglosphere, even the best speakers can lack confidence in their English. They may worry that their accents will be laughed at (and unfortunately, they're not completely wrong).

Let's not abandoned all hope. Video is a compelling medium, but we need to have realistic expectations about costs and timelines.

For more detailed advice, I recommend Ohlsen's two free books on the production process for international media. Although intended for media production and translation companies, if you're considering global corporate video, both *Insider's Guide To The Foreign Language Video Marketplace*[37] and *Insider's Guide to Translating Foreign Language Video*[36] contain good advice and resources.

Visualize a different way

Despite the challenges outlined in this chapter, visuals are a powerful way to extend your reach around the world and create memorable messages.[23] In *Visual Literacy*[8], Dr. Lynell Burmark writes "…unless our words, concepts, ideas are hooked onto an image, they will go in one ear, sail through the brain, and go out the other ear. Words are processed by our short-term memory where we can only retain about seven bits of information (plus or minus 2)…. Images, on the other hand, go directly into long-term memory where they are indelibly etched."

These principles apply to all employees, and if visuals are done well and culturally localized, they can be a cost-effective way to inspire and change behaviors.

---

[2] "3 Reasons to Liven Up Your Marketing with Visual Content"[9].

[3] ChangingMinds.org [http://changingminds.org/explanations/learning/active_learning.htm] cited research that users retained just 10% of written information after three days, compared to 65% of information presented visually and verbally[11].

CHAPTER 5
Local Communicators

When Corporate Communications pushes global content to local markets, they may offer instructions as guidance, expecting that local staff will use their best judgment and adapt those instructions to make the content more effective for their locale.

Because that expectation isn't always understood or agreed upon, the regions and countries often defer to corporate's instructions, either following them precisely or ignoring them if they decide the content is irrelevant to their business model.

Corporate often fails to grasp that adapting content requires skills that aren't always readily available to local teams. Most global communication departments don't have dedicated resources in each country with reporting lines back to them. Instead, they have informal contacts who deploy deliverables and feed results back. Because reporting lines are informal, most internal communication managers call this their *network*.

Informants might be a better description. These contacts have primary responsibilities inside their own departments, and someone other than Communications manages them. Each network member's interactions with the corporate office is limited, and they aren't likely to know their counterparts elsewhere in the network. Since they are often only partially dedicated to communications, they're hard to train. For example, because they post new content so infrequently, they may have to re-learn the publishing tool each time they use it. As you might expect, their formal communication skills can vary considerably.

Local leaders don't always see a convincing need to invest in communication resources. In settings where the communication role isn't valued or understood, people assigned to it have often, as one senior consultant put it, "failed into the role."

Due to a widespread belief among business people that anyone can do communications, managers might assign people they no longer want to work with or young hires they intend to groom for other roles. Local communications teams might get assigned a high-potential hire in human resources, but that person's interest often remains with recruiting, learning, or community involvement, and communications rarely gets the focus it needs.

It's hard on those tapped if they're not meant for the role. I was once part of a team that was forced to take on somebody ousted from a regional marketing group. He was a skilled photographer and a talented event organizer, and in some communication departments he would have been a good fit. Unfortunately, at that time we needed written content. Expecting him to take on quality control for verbal content was a huge struggle and ultimately frustrating for both him and the rest of the team. Happily, he eventually landed another job with better prospects, but his time with us left him feeling discouraged.

Countries assign people to communications for various reasons, including expediency, and corporate makes optimistic assumptions about the network's motivations and abilities, thinking the capabilities of each locale are the same. It doesn't help that corporate often knows its network contacts only by name and email, and when they find out weeks later that a person has moved on, they just update the distribution list without bothering to learn anything about the replacement.

If you want to move forward with a localization program, you need to get personally acquainted with the network. Elevating the status of local communications is both a cultural and tactical shift, and it will take time, so look first at what skills practitioners in the network are likely to have at the outset. As you groom and build your local network, you should assess members and their aspirations individually.

Until you get to know them better, you can anticipate that network members will fit into one of three categories, depending on market size (small, medium, and large).

Resource capabilities in small, medium, and large markets

Small markets

In markets where your company presence is small, your main contact is probably the country's chief executive. That has some advantages, because country heads more easily grasp business objectives and are more likely to understand how an initiative supports their interests. Some will do exactly as you request, engaging with content and deploying it in ways appropriate to that market.

However, most will not. They will pass execution on to someone else, probably someone unknown to you. This means you have only indirect control over the instructions. If that messenger is an administrative assistant (a common scenario), he or she may not appreciate that you need their support to deliver content with impact. Your instructions will be followed to the letter and no more. The chances are just about zero that a random communicator assigned to the task will have adequate skills or training to deploy content creatively with opportunity for feedback and dialogue.

Medium-sized markets

Middle-tier markets may have someone dedicated at least partially to internal communications, and it's likely a slightly higher position. But it's often someone from human resources or marketing who has additional responsibilities. They are often known members of the network, someone informally assigned to corporate, with all kinds of ambiguity and political strings attached.

People in this position might have more experience than their counterparts in smaller markets, but their main job takes higher priority. They may have some useful skills, but if they are only 20% dedicated to communications, it's hard to train them effectively on tools they rarely use. Like the administrative assistants in the smaller markets, they probably want to scratch your tasks off their to-do list quickly, and they may think they can address an issue with a single, all-employee email message.

If their relationship to you remains informal year after year, they have little motivation to develop skills and improve processes. I've seen people in these roles exhausted over time and made cynical by too many centralized, ineffective global deliverables with no incentive or time to improve them. In these cases, they too will follow corporate instructions to the letter and will fail to adapt content with the critical eye and flexibility that you're hoping for.

Large markets

In these countries, your company has probably invested more in personnel and they're more likely to have an experienced communicator. These people are probably better known to the corporate team, and you may have even hired them. This may give you more peace of mind, but success isn't certain.

Just as anywhere, the skills of communicators in large markets can vary, depending on the company's investment in that market. They may dedicate more of their time to employee communications, and they may even have a clear reporting line to you. But you can't always expect dynamic, state-of-the art execution.

In practice, they may not have the authority to push back on, for instance, a local leader's insistence on an ineffective campaign.[1] Or they may have started their career in departments like labor or *health and safety (H&S)* and their daily practices are still rooted in those legacy priorities. Or they may have a content delivery channel that they're stubbornly wedded to, such as a local newsletter whose performance has never been measured. These are all worst-case scenarios, but they're fairly common. Language barriers fortify the walls of fiefdoms, and it's easy for those on the inside to resist change.

Common network skills and limitations

Local investment for communications is typically kept minimal, and I've emphasized pitfalls because they can be common. These pitfalls can also

---

[1] Power dynamics often put communicators low on the organizational hierarchy ("Understanding Power Dynamics Will Make You More Persuasive"[18]).

linger over the long term, because keeping people up to date on tools like a *CMS* can be especially difficult if they are only partially dedicated to communications and use it only once a quarter.[2]

But these pitfalls aren't universal. A high performer for Communications can come from anywhere. You may find someone with a related degree and aspirations to grow with the company, or someone who has already been blogging or moderating a social media group. Developing people with skills and interests like these is a good first step for your localization/co-creation program. But you won't learn of the possibility unless you get to know your network personally.

Before you set out on localization and co-creation, you must understand your network members' strengths, weaknesses, and aspirations so that you can tailor content and briefings that are more useful to them.

Listen to your major markets

With Germany's economic power and size, German is often one of the first European languages in which companies invest. But the complexity of the country's regulations, customs, and preferences make it among the most difficult for corporate employee communications to penetrate.

In much of Europe, change in workplace conditions—which includes asking employees to use an app or changing how they log into a workplace portal—must be negotiated with in-country *works councils*. Works councils are employee-led representative bodies. They rarely have veto power over what companies do, but changes must be reviewed with them first, which can take weeks and even months in some cases.

Works councils are especially time consuming in the German-speaking countries of Germany, Austria, and Switzerland. Many companies refer to these countries as DACH, an acronym formed by their country-name ISO designations (D – Germany, A – Austria, CH – Switzerland).

---

[2] Foster's Simplified User Interface could enable better training for occasional users [20]. See the section titled "Assessing and prioritizing costs for translations" (p. 110) for more.

If you combine works councils with the people of DACH's reluctance to adopt social media, electronic payments, or buying online from sites that aren't domestic, you quickly end up with workarounds (for example, "All employees can submit questions anonymously through this URL, except in Germany, Austria, and Switzerland where they can…"). These awkward, temporary solutions can drag on for months.

If Germany is central in your company's European growth plans, DACH is likely one of the first places you'll try localization. With their strong local preferences and economic heft, your German organization likely has someone executing communications. You must tap into their knowledge of local conditions. Even if they're in functions outside communications, such as operations, labor relations, or human resources, they understand the differences between the three DACH countries and your company's stake in each. That makes them good candidates to execute communications in partnership with local business units.

Part I Conclusion

Despite business borders that seem continually more open, our contemporary landscape has subtle barriers to communicating with employees worldwide. You can change this landscape for the better, but you must get both corporate and local business units committed to communicating better. You'll have to get to know and trust each other, which is easier if you're continually having conversations not just about content but also about business drivers.

The regions have to show corporate that they're competent and can create and execute work appropriately, while corporate must demonstrate that it can grasp local business realities and help overcome challenges. Better campaigns in local settings hinge on both happening, repeatedly and over time, through open and ongoing dialogue about goals and tactics.

Leadership, Governance, and Budget

Localization and co-creation of employee communications represent a change from conventional processes. Formalizing these practices and making them operational requires attention from corporate, local commitment, and backing from global and local leadership.

What You'll Learn: The decisions you need to make and the support you need in order to create an organization capable of localization and co-creation.

Why You Should Care: You can't force localization, and chances for success are low without support from leadership and the right stakeholders.

CHAPTER 6
Setting the Stage

To successfully localize, you need to earn agreement among corporate and local stakeholders. Corporate Communications can't do this on its own. By advancing internal localization and co-creation, you also advance internal communications. Even if the company is unwilling to invest significantly, you can pilot localization in a few markets with the resources you already have. This part examines the underlying decisions you need to make first and what kind of future investments you should consider.

No matter the scale of localization you attempt, you need a clear view of your company's global structure for communications. Your company's industry and culture will help you determine which approach—or more likely, which mix of approaches—is best.

Globalizing communications should become more than a capability, it should become your modus operandi, and no matter where you implement it, you'll be building a process that will evolve.

The struggle for resources

Some organizations invest in employee communications because they know it drives business. A senior communications manager with a global industrial company told me that an internal audit at his company found that the locations with the most effective employee communications also happened to be the most profitable.

His findings weren't widely known within the company, which isn't surprising since that correlation isn't understood in business generally. Instead, management sees employee communications as a cost center—and a luxury expense—that they'd prefer to keep small. Even in startups, internal communications is seldom top of mind.

The employee communications profession commonly complains about inadequate funding and lack of leadership support. At times the job feels like you're part of a typing pool, completely reactive to requests from people who have more power but who are less aware of best practices. In our conferences, workshops, and blogs a typical topic is, "how can we get a seat at the table?" We speculate that with more power, we'd be able to intervene in time to prevent bad decisions in communications.

In fact, we are relatively close to power, but locally we miss the mark. Despite our complaints about no place at the table, Corporate Communications tends to become a megaphone, an Ivory Tower function disseminating executive talking points.

Leaders in the profession say that our struggle for attention has less to do with access to power and more to do with our distance from the business. "The farther you get away from the center of a company, the more complicated things become," said one senior communications consultant in Chicago. "Business unit leaders want their communications teams talking about what drives their bonuses. These motivations are compounded by geography, which makes it more difficult to deploy consistent messaging."

A localization program is a chance to improve communication for the better. When local business units take an active role in communicating, they are more committed to an outcome and less likely to simply blame corporate.

Management will want to see return on investment, so you must to be ready to prove the value of localization. You need to use localized communications to address local pain points, or they will never agree to the additional effort.

> Genuine localization and co-creation adds complexity to the process of employee communications, but it gives it a huge boost in credibility by closing the gap between Corporate Communications and the business.

Justifying the need for localization

Corporate sometimes sneaks questions into surveys to find out if people recognize mission statements and other strategic mantras. The results are often frustrating to them.

That frustration can persuade top executives to pay more attention to localization. But if the primary driver is about adoption of corporate priorities, local business units won't rally behind the expensive and time-consuming processes of translation, localization, or co-creation. These processes must serve local interests too.

If you show local businesses how low engagement with content undermines their goals, they may be more willing to pitch in and localize. Look at employee performance measures that are important to them, such as absenteeism, recruiting, retention, and safety, as well as sales goals such as selling the right products to the right customers or building new capabilities for targeted industries. Localization should help managers communicate with their teams, so follow up to learn whether it contributes to engagement, performance, and the bottom line.

> If a business unit isn't meeting its goals or its results are declining, localization can help them turn things around. Localization commits them to the goal of communicating effectively and delivering content that has an impact.

Resources in place for crises

In order to effectively manage the non-stop, 24-hour media cycle, organizations can no longer keep communications entirely centralized. "Despite the immediacy of social media, we're relying on instinct," said the Chicago-based consultant. "If the Beijing government says something that your company needs to speak to while the head office is asleep, you need people on the ground smart enough to react. You need the right people with the right skill sets."

Having someone who coordinates communications across internal and external channels will improve responsiveness and mitigate risk both during a crisis as well as day-to-day. Bringing local businesses into communications planning is a good start. "We in Corporate Communications have to decide what we want to be talking about this quarter, this month, this day," he said. "What does the 12-month plan look like? What is our view of the likely issues? We can prepare material ahead of time and nurture people locally who know how to tweak it."

If senior leaders are stuck in the mindset that communications people are their typing pool—that corporate sends and employees receive—localization will look like an unnecessary expense. On the other hand, if they want a consistent customer experience across all channels and locations, if they want their brand to evoke a certain feeling in customers and employees, or if they want clarity on issues like global policies, procedures, and brand use, they need local people skilled in communications.

Above all, greater localization can be pitched as a way to get more from what's already being spent on various types of corporate content. Ann Rockley, CEO of Toronto-based The Rockley Group, Inc., is a leading expert in intelligent content strategy and best practices in content management. The Rockley Group helps organizations move toward structured strategies in content management and dynamic publishing.

In an interview, Rockley said that rather than handcrafting content piece-by-piece as most communications departments do, content re-purposing helps organizations get more from the money they're spending. "We can do more with the same number of people. When you re-use content, it's like gaining people, gaining time, gaining reach. There is never enough time or money for internal information, and that's always a necessary evil. You can optimize what you're doing and therefore do more of it, and better. That's the business case."

Finding a leader

Whether you move toward translation, localization, or co-creation, a leader responsible for the program is critical. One senior communications manager told me that soon after his US-based employer signed with a global language service provider (LSP), a business unit hired its own vendor. While the local invoice was lower than what the LSP would have charged, the savings was negated because the company couldn't reach the LSP's contracted minimum, triggering a new set of charges.

"Since we don't have a person overseeing the process, it's the Wild West," he said. "Companies on the higher end of the maturity scale have well-established processes in place, but more importantly, they have someone with the trust, knowledge and authority to drive it. Translation, localization, or whatever you call it, if one person doesn't take ownership of the whole concept, it's going to be impossible to nail."

Reporting lines for global communication teams

Those executing local employee communications often work on their own, with only a loose association with Corporate Communications. It's time to overcome this barrier and create one sense of purpose, bringing together skill sets, budget, and technology.

Achieving localization is far easier if the organization sees the reporting line to Corporate Communications as solid. If there must be a secondary (dotted line) reporting structure, it should be to the geography or business unit. Yet an effective global network requires more than drawing lines on org charts. Your team should be structured to support mature localization and co-creation processes and to strengthen those processes over time.

"Business environments change and the communications function changes as well," said the Chicago consultant. "We must ask ourselves what skill sets the communications team has, and what our dedication to their professional development is. There's a strong need to drive skill sets and be smart about who's on the team."

Once in place, Communications must be ready to step up for its network members. "The head of communications needs to commit to the local business that they'll get a sophisticated level of support, one that's better than they had before. That means a commitment to having the right people in the right roles. It means having a professionalized career structure within communications and investing in people and their skill sets. There should be room for personal advancement and growth, with a solid line back into the center," he said.

Evaluating costs, benefits, and who pays

If corporate is paying for it, you'd think that bringing new talent into local business units would be welcome, but adding resources can be surprisingly controversial. If you decide from on high that local businesses need these capabilities and then impose your decision, it could be dismissed as just another unhelpful idea from corporate. That would be a tough environment to place a communicator in.

In larger countries that have full-time employee communications staff, that debate may have already been settled. But it can still be an issue in smaller countries. If local leaders think they're getting along without communications staff, and neither corporate nor local business units are willing to increase their payroll, the result may be a stalemate and an extension of the status quo.

To succeed, you need to build the business case for localization with stakeholders at both the corporate office and the business units.

What Corporate Communications gets from its network

Consistent messaging has long been a goal of communication departments, but most practitioners in marketing, public relations, and employee communications are so focused on their sphere of work that they don't follow up to see if their colleagues adapt or make use of the content they produce. This is especially true in larger companies with high levels of specialization.[1]

As communication channels continue to multiply and fragment, the communications function needs to try harder to coordinate messaging across all its disciplines. Investing in localization is a great opportunity to align efforts and unify messaging.

How such coordination works will depend on the market. In larger markets, an empowered employee communications function can leverage localized marketing and public relations deliverables, giving that content more reach

---

[1] Nobody in Communications is against coordinated output, but organizations are frustratingly siloed, and cross-disciplinary planning calendars that work are surprisingly rare.

and exposure. In smaller markets, coordinating and re-purposing content should be easier because probably just one person is responsible.

What business units get from a localization network

In large markets, you may already have communicators in place, and they likely report to local executives. These leaders must be convinced that corporate involvement will not undermine their influence and that they'll get a sophisticated level of support, better than they had before. Improved visuals and better coordination with global announcements are good proof points.

In smaller markets where you're proposing new resources, your case may be more convincing if the role integrates communications activities across marketing, public relations, and social media. Additional help in those three areas is something business units are often more open to because they're perceived as sales enabling and revenue generating.

Moreover, an integrated role in smaller markets may be easier to fill. Capable communicators with strong language skills are in demand in those markets, and they may be attracted to a broader role.

What business units can expect

Since many businesses aren't sold on the value of communications, once your localization program is under way you'll want to push for quick wins.

A capable network should support local business units with more than content. They should provide advice to various functions on how to reach local audiences, how to have positive, measurable impact on business performance, and how to contribute to local brand reputation.

If possible, at least partial local ownership of content localization is preferable. When they invest their own money, local business units begin looking at ways to enhance and optimize their communications budget.

However, until local business units experience effective communications support first hand, their leaders will see localization staff as creators of emails, articles and newsletters. That view lessens the potential of local communications and puts them at risk during cutbacks. They will see the activity as a line-item expense, something nice-to-have but not essential (and easily cut).

As business units buy in, their input into the process grows. Local executives may be more willing, for example, to meet regularly with your network contact or invest in training and additional resources.

However, if the local executives persist in the belief that investing in communications doesn't help the business, then consider bringing in a local person who reports directly to you. Having someone formally on your team, administered and funded by corporate, puts those activities and expenses in a central, global budget.

Over time, communications activities will demonstrate value to business units, and those benefits should reduce resistance to allocating communications expenses to their budgets. In more mature markets, you may be moving toward co-creation already. If markets are evolving in that direction, the argument for local financial support becomes stronger.

Challenges to building a new network

When you create a new local role, it's important to understand that the journey is just beginning. Unless the person is highly experienced, you won't be able to just drop them in country and assume all will be well. You must continue to develop people's capabilities, do your best to retain them, and fend off low-value, inconsequential projects.

In markets with an integrated role, network resources will be under continual pressure from leaders to focus on external communications, and some communicators will prefer those activities. An ongoing difficulty with an integrated, cross-disciplinary role is ensuring that the right amount of attention gets paid to employee communications. I've seen local management push communications staff from 50% dedicated to internal communications to practically zero. To claim that time, you and your local network contact must continually make the case that better employee communications has a positive impact on revenue and costs.

What managers need to understand about communicating globally

Mid-level managers at corporate must understand investment in localization. They often see preparing content for international markets as icing on a cake, an afterthought that's nice to have, but not always necessary.

Global departments need to understand the language needs of their internal stakeholders, which countries their initiatives affect, and the extent of the impact. Mid-level managers need to apply this awareness to every project plan and set reasonable timelines. They need to know when they need local-language content and how to develop that content without it becoming an expensive, last-minute rush job.

Old habits die hard, and this is no small task for large companies. In her 2014 PhD thesis, *Intercultural competences needed by global CEOs*[21], Barbara Gibson wrote that companies that become multinational over time struggle with cultural nuance, while startups with international ambitions often operate more effectively in multiple markets from the beginning.

If a company is operating in four or more countries within three years of startup, Gibson calls them *born global*. Managers in such startups are often more agile in handling local variations because their strategy was global from the start.

Educating management in larger, more established organizations is a longer undertaking. The communications manager I cited earlier, the one who led his global employer's selection of a single translation vendor, said their challenges didn't end with the work agreement.

"Once onboard, our vendor told us that most of our problem was human, and they were right. Different business units and countries all had their preferred local vendors. Project managers didn't know which language sets they needed, and they didn't understand how to provide content to translators so that it was timely and used correct terminology."

By now his company is further along its path to better international content, but he said that human misunderstandings of what, how, and when to translate keep reappearing. "They think of me as the translations guy, and I get ridiculous questions from product managers. When they roll out products in new countries, they come and ask me which languages they need to translate into. Don't they have people in their own group who can tell them?"

Tying localization to business outcomes

Both corporate and local leadership should understand how translation and localization works. Rosie Halfhead, a London-based consultant in brand, strategy, marketing, sales and stakeholder engagement, told me about a client's inter-regional misunderstanding that she turned into an opportunity for localization.

The company's headquarters had agreed to sponsor a conference in Asia and then handed tactical responsibility over to the region. The region didn't see the relevance of the event, and at the last minute it quickly produced local collateral to be used alongside what was shipped from headquarters. The result was brand and messaging confusion, and neither side was happy.

To prevent such mishaps in the future, she went to the leadership of local business units to discuss their needs. Among other things, she learned that they wanted more locally relevant case studies in languages of the region.

She followed up by organizing a workshop for Asian country managers to develop these new case studies, and at the same time, foster a more coherent use of the brand in the region.

"We took corporate's top three messages and then broke them down to different business areas. We discussed what each meant for Japan, Singapore, and so on. The country managers then saw linkages between what they were doing to prioritize their activities and how they linked to the company overall."

After the workshop, country managers provided specific, local proof points of global strategy, and Communications polished them up into finished case studies. As a result, regions were more able to present themselves with geographic relevance.

Halfhead added that the workshop had longer-term benefits, including the empowerment of her regional communication teams. For many companies, local communicators are beholden to local leadership, regardless of reporting lines, and they're routinely coerced into executing low-value projects with little power to propose alternatives.

In the weeks that followed the workshop, now with the country managers' understanding and support, her team conducted an audit of local collateral. "We did it ourselves with a spreadsheet, asking about costs, objectives, resource commitment, and impact assessments. It wasn't that sophisticated, but we quickly saw what mattered and what didn't," she said. "It allowed our local teams to just stop doing stuff that had less value."

> Many companies see a wide gap between the business and what many call the Ivory Tower. Localization helps close that gap.

By working with and educating leaders, Halfhead forged a tighter bond between them and her local communications network. That bond is especially important if the local culture is hierarchical and there is a wide separation between leaders and junior communicators, which in my experience, includes most organizations. At the same time, she sharpened her communicators' critical skills and showed them how to prioritize and keep their focus on business needs. "It's important to encourage and empower local practitioners to continually ask why," she said.

Imagining a better intranet

In 2018, Gartner updated *How to Select the Intranet Foundation for Your Digital Workplace*[39], putting intranet capabilities into three categories: destination intranet, distributed intranet, and network of work. Distributed intranet and network of work are aspirational for most, and they complement the mobile and cloud technologies that are changing ways of working.

The destination intranet—one that people must go out of their way to visit—is the most traditional. It has company strategy and company news, and in my experience, it's the most common. Most organizations have been maintaining destination intranets since they launched their first one in the late 1990s, and they've been complaining about readership ever since.

Architects of intranets recommend plenty of research into user preferences and behavior, but from what I've seen, English seems to be the only language considered. Perhaps because the intranet is a destination, the interests or needs of global users are rarely taken into account. Unfortunately, employees are often stuck with these decisions for years.[2]

In an interview, Gerry McGovern, founder and CEO of Customer Carewords and an expert on digital customer experience, confirmed that multilingual intranets are rare. "Most intranets are seriously neglected and they can't manage one language properly. There may be local content, but it's probably not well organized. Organizations will often invest in technology but not in maintenance. The tools they have are already quite good. We have more than enough tools. What we don't have are people intelligent enough to use them."

If you want to make you intranet more useful, you need to address multiple user needs. Language capabilities are among them. Content language options for destination intranets can be put into three categories:

- **English-only:** As Jonathan Phillips noted in Chapter 1, the user base for English-only intranets generally doesn't extend beyond global/regional offices and English-speaking countries. If you don't believe him or me, and you're not measuring your own global usage, now is the time to start. Expending energy on content that you're not even sure is being consumed makes no sense, yet I frequently see companies blindly assuming that employees seek out company news. Unless there's content that global employees must access to do their jobs, very few are going to take time to explore it.

- **A blend of English and local language:** Many CMSs allow you to mix global and local-language content. Local HR and other functions may post forms and documents in the local language, particularly if it's

---

[2] This is a widespread problem. One survey, "Intranet Search Is More Than a Technology Problem"[61], found that 64 percent of intranets were available in only one language.

legally mandated. But multilingual CMS capabilities are rarely used for feature content because managing multiple-language versions isn't easy.

"Managing multilingual intranets is a slice and dice of language and location," said Phillips. "Many companies run a system that knows where you're based and knows your language setting, or maybe a field in an *Active Directory* can select content so that you see what you should be seeing."

This requires accurate demographic data on employees, but location-based blending of global and local content creates problems for users. For example, a US employee traveling in Italy probably doesn't want Italian content.

"For a manager hired in the UK but working an assignment abroad, the question becomes what do you serve up, UK or local content? In international businesses where people move around for months at a time, an approach using only data isn't going to work. In these situations, we ask users to choose language or locale, and then they see content tailored to their choice," said Phillips.

It's tempting to assume that employees in Germany want German, and those in Russia want Russian, but at the November 2017 LocWorld 35 conference, Jon Ann Lindsey of Google and Val Swisher of Content Rules presented a case study ("Optimizing Content in the Real World at Google"[32]) that found this not to be true. You need to get feedback from users "before you make decisions about how you'll translate and localize content."

A language mix for intranets also calls for well-trained authors. Feeding your intranet with relevant local content—and tagging it with metadata to enable search—requires an investment in time, tools, and training. If you rely on automated filtering instead of a local, human curator, user experience will quickly become a jumble of outdated and not very useful content.

- **All local-language content:** This kind of intranet would essentially be multiple, single-country or single-language intranets. Authors would have more responsibility to curate and augment content, maintain user experience, and be accurate. While this could be an ideal approach, it could also be overly complex and expensive.

"Huge companies may be able to serve up unique content, but they're overcomplicating it," said Phillips, who advocates a process of localization and co-creation that can be done relatively easily using the drafting and publishing modes of most CMSs.

"Corporate teams write content authored in English that can eventually be published across the company. The content is written, sent for translation, and saved as a draft on local intranets. Local teams can review it, make sure it's good for their audience, and publish," he said. "You have to be comfortable with their minor edits. If you've hired a translation agency to translate into Parisian French, that content might not be okay with all French-speaking locations. The best thing is to always allow local teams to polish and make it their own."[3]

In Chapter 1, Phillips warned that information *material* to a public company's stock price should have a process of its own, and local teams must understand that localizing and revising such content can cause major problems.

As McGovern noted, companies struggle to maintain a useful intranet in one language, and they don't take on additional languages for a good reason: it's hard. But it is possible. To improve an intranet's usability, he said you don't need a lot of people, but you need people who are skilled.

"It's better to have a few skilled resources than hundreds of contributors who publish only occasionally," he said. "The intranets that are real disasters have hundreds of publishers who have each had a half-day's training on SharePoint. The better-managed ones have smaller, tighter teams that maintain quality, people who are skilled at writing web content, information architecture and user experience. Those skills are difficult to build up in

---

[3] Valo, a consultancy specializing in SharePoint intranets, has a blog post ("Multilingual intranets: Automating your localization process with Microsoft Flow and Translator"[29]) about this localizing process using SharePoint, Microsoft Flow, and Microsoft Translator.

people if they dedicate just five to fifteen percent of their time to contributing to the intranet."

> We need people outside of corporate headquarters who have the ability to shape and create content, monitor user experience, assess global content, and remove what's outdated and irrelevant.

The dispersed intranet team should have autonomy to create and curate content, otherwise Corporate Communications will get overwhelmed with requests to filter or expire content. However, as McGovern pointed out, you need to manage this process for those that do it infrequently. Permissions for local authors should depend on the maturity of your network and their degree of dedication to Communications.

One technological capability that could help localize some parts of your intranet experience is a *component content management system (CCMS)*—a centralized system that manages content as re-usable components. A CCMS provides structured content, and if you can combine one with a terminology management system (TMS), machine translation, and *translation memory* tools, it will be easier for you to produce, adapt, manage, and deliver content in multiple languages. These combined capabilities are what Swisher calls the "Holy Trifecta"[56].

Yet even with advanced tools, maintenance and curation is still largely a human task. This is an area where a regional team offering intranet maintenance may work best.

For CMS authors who are fully dedicated members of your network and who are trained on your tools' multilingual capabilities, an evolution toward co-creation is inevitable.

Intranet measurement

In Chapter 2, I outlined some challenges in comparing data from international locations. In Chapter 17, I look at outcomes your localization program could measure. Intranet measurement though, deserves its own discussion.

Since the user experience for most intranets is poor, it can make sense to undertake an intranet cleanup project. Such a project can give you the opportunity to incorporate localization practices, but making an intranet effective will take much more than curating your content mix.

Intranet measurement is commonly ineffective. Either companies don't measure usage at all or they become fixated on spikes and dips in page views. Both approaches reinforce the conventional practice of creating more (little read) content.

McGovern developed Top Tasks Management, a research and management model to help large organizations improve customer experience through identifying and optimizing top tasks of customers.

His company, Customer Carewords, applied the model to intranets, surveying 49,000 employees in 55 organizations. They found that employees most frequently looked for content in four categories—News/Current Affairs, About Me, About the Company, and Find People/Collaboration. Communication departments typically focus on only one of these: News/Current Affairs. In a blog post ("Intranet in a Box"[30]), they recommend combining these four with core user tasks. Looking at your own usage data in this way, you can plan how to improve your intranet.

The post concludes, "So do we have an Intranet in a Box, ready to go? Not quite, but it's certainly a good start. Without doubt, the best intranets are built by those who view them in a logical way, based on data of what employees actually need to do."

In our interview, McGovern said, "Start by understanding what your staff wants to do most and then make it easy to for them to do it. Then you build credibility. For example, a carmaker might know CAD engine drawings are critical and yet they're having a hard time finding the right ones. If you can make it faster and easier for engineers to find them, then you get their attention. You can prove that you're really helping reduce defects or raise productivity. Focus on the top tasks of employees, as defined by them. Make a discernible improvement in that, and then people begin to understand the promise of digital."

The issue of intranet measurement has also appeared in the research of Netherlands-based consultant Mike Klein ("How to measure what really matters"[26]). He interviewed participating internal communications practitioners around the world to learn about "the issues they face in identifying, collecting, analyzing, and convincingly presenting relevant data to their stakeholders."

Many practitioners voiced concern that measurement for engagement and page views doesn't really tell them much that they can act on. Moreover, such numbers don't tell you whether users were successful in accessing the content they wanted or whether they understood it, shared it, stored it, printed it, or took some action with it.

Klein writes that measuring enterprise search in "digital workspaces, social intranets, or Enterprise Social Networks," has great potential in "assessing relevance and sentiment."

"The power of enterprise search as an employee data source is that the data is both quantitative and qualitative. Not only can the popularity of search terms be identified, but the prevalence of alternative terminology ('performance optimization' vs. 'cost cutting') can be assessed. In some cases, search term usage can be analyzed geographically and even demographically."

Unfortunately, search functionality in intranets rarely gets good reviews, and such measurements may not be available. If you can measure intranet search, the data can help show you where to focus localization efforts.

Martin White wrote that whether corporate realizes it or not, sought-after content is often in a language other than English. "...while English may be the default corporate language, the intranet is a core repository for content that is local in scope and language." He continues, saying that the languages of your employees' search terms may be revealing. "...if you operate outside of countries which have English as their national language, then you are certainly going to have content in at least two, if not more, languages. Does your search functionality provide equivalent levels of performance in each language? If not, why not?"[4]

---

[4] "Intranet Search Is More Than a Technology Problem"[61].

However, when looking at search metrics, know that most users have given up using their intranet's search function because it doesn't work well. Instead, they navigate from memory or rely on bookmarks.

McGovern points out that as a result, "So many people have given up on search that you're not getting insight, you're getting exceptional behavior. If you can get the analytics, you need to be careful with interpreting them. It's strange that everyone understands the value of Google and the importance of search, but for their intranet, they don't give a damn. If nobody is putting metadata on content, search isn't going to work very well. It requires decent editorial quality and management, information design, maintenance of metadata, and removal of old content. These basics are missing in a lot of intranets."

CHAPTER 7
Localization Models

Examples of localization are easier to come by in branded channels. Every year since 2004, John Yunker has published a web globalization report,[1] an assessment of websites for 150 global brands.

If there's a list that long of the best global internal sites, I've never seen it. Marketing is much further along in developing an online presence across cultures. Employee communications should look to these leading external websites to learn how they present themselves and earn loyalty. Their best practices can help you start thinking about how to manage content for employee communications across markets and cultures.

One interesting aspect of Yunker's research is that once marketers start localization, they tend to expand it. In the 2019 edition, Yunker wrote that over the last 15 years, the average number of languages supported in the top 150 sites has more than doubled to 33. A localization program for employees may also expand to more languages over time.

In this chapter I explore four models of brand management, provided to me by two senior advertising and brand consultants in Chicago. The models range from traditional and centralized to liberal and decentralized.

For each model, I outline the example, then describe basic features relevant to employee communications. I point out the kinds of companies or business units that each model might be suitable for, and I propose how it can be implemented and pitfalls to look out for.

---

[1] As of this writing, the latest is *The 2019 Web Globalization Report Card*[65].

Table 7.1 – Four models of brand management

Centrally Managed		Autonomous Teams	
Limited Flexibility	Greater Flexibility	Strong Guidance	Minimal Guidance
← Greater central control — Greater autonomy →			

Each model requires different preparation and investment, and each might succeed or struggle depending on your size, industry, and brand standards. In practice, a system for global communication will likely be a mix of these. A decentralized model might be better for mature business units, while centrally sourced content might be better for newer, smaller business units.

Localization practices vary by location and evolve over time, so knowing the strengths and weaknesses of each model can help you anticipate risks and get the most from what you implement.

Centrally managed teams with limited flexibility

Centrally Managed		Autonomous Teams	
Limited Flexibility	Greater Flexibility	Strong Guidance	Minimal Guidance
← Greater central control — Greater autonomy →			

Whenever I talk to designers experienced in global campaigns, the first localization option they describe involves multiple language versions created centrally at Corporate, perhaps supplemented by simple templates for commonly needed deliverables. The extent to which local business units can alter these templates depends on the program's maturity.

The primary benefit to this approach is a sense of unity. It's a controlled model that's a logical starting point for traditionally minded businesses that want some global control. It's often deployed by bigger companies and those that became global over time.

Example: niche B2B manufacturer with a small budget

For companies with commoditized offerings, brand recognition doesn't necessarily drive sales. One global chemical company was well known in its space, and marketing energy was devoted to developing new products. It was up to regional offices to maintain contact with customers, regulators, and other stakeholders.

Its brand needs were simple: be consistent, reliable, and easy for local business units to use. One of the brand consultants told me, "An out-of-control brand is meaningless. If materials have many different looks, the company seems disorganized. In more rules-bound companies, Corporate wants to maintain consistency, while on the local side, resources are limited and they want to be told what to do. They don't want to spend time on co-creation. It's a matter of simplicity."

Where to implement this model

Local business units whose operating model is largely the same everywhere can function well with strict, rules-based brand guidelines. It's best for companies or business units that don't have creative resources on site or don't want to spend resources altering content. Companies in this position don't obsess about creative details and don't insist on their own unique visuals. They will be happy with appealing and easy-to-use templates.

Pitfalls and how to mitigate them

Risk: templates are too hard to use or are unappealing

If people find templates too complicated to work with, they create unique, non-compliant materials on their own that violate brand standards. Standard corporate slide decks tend to be bloated, catch-all templates with hundreds of slide models—intro slides, transitions, graph styles. Most people don't need or want the full range of styles. Instead of making sure they have the latest version of the template, they open their most recent presentation, duplicate it, and start revising. As a result, their creative choices end up looking the same month after month, and it's hard to keep them up to date on revisions to the corporate template.

What to do about it: For templates to work, you need to apply *user-centered design* principles (see Chapter 10). Find out how employees intend to use them, what tools they have, and what features they need.

Risk: sites have different needs

Don't presume locations are the same when in fact they're quite different. Even if your worldwide product offerings are mostly the same, the local customer base and resourcing model can result in different employee demographics with different needs and interests. In a chemical company for example, one facility may have more automation than another and be staffed by fewer, more highly trained people.

Local target customers can also affect employee needs. The company might be pursuing high-end carmakers in Europe, but targeting manufacturers of small appliances in Asia. Such differences can mean that the message for employees needs to be different.

What to do about it: Make it easy to change text content but equally easy to preserve style elements such as the *font family*. For translations, set aside time for in-country reviews.

Risk: demand for creative resources is too high

If you provide access to centralized creative services for more advanced needs, those resources can easily become overwhelmed by local demand for microsites, presentations, newsletters, and video. If those services can't keep up, or if the local business units feel that the costs being charged back to them are too high, they'll do it on their own, potentially resulting in ugly, off-brand, and ineffective local work.

What to do about it: If you have an exacting brand, provide low-cost access to creative services. Alternatively, make templates easy to adapt. Either way, offer frequent user training workshops where they get practical experience. What designers find intuitive can be confusing to others.

Summary

Strengths:

- Enables more consistent use of brand visuals
- Streamlines use of creative resources
- Saves local markets time by relieving demands for local resources

Weaknesses:

- Less tailorable for unique market needs
- Global messaging could fall flat, or communications deliverables could go unused if not a perfect fit

Which organizations or business units it's best suited for:

- Where unique local visual expression of the brand is less essential
- Where the volume of creative demand is manageable
- Where business units have access to global/regional resources for creative deliverables

Whose budget: Creative resources are likely managed regionally or at Corporate. However, since the brand is managed centrally and similar everywhere, costs can be shared among business units.

Centrally managed teams with greater flexibility

Centrally Managed		Autonomous Teams	
Limited Flexibility	Greater Flexibility	Strong Guidance	Minimal Guidance
← Greater central control — Greater autonomy →			

Providing a mix of templates and brand guidelines is the most common way to give a centrally managed team greater flexibility, especially following a brand refresh or new identity. For many companies though, creating content according to guidelines is more aspirational than practical.

Example: technology company with hundreds of products

A prominent technology brand with hundreds of different products in many countries hired an agency to create flexible assets that local business units could assemble and re-purpose more autonomously. The agency provided detailed guidelines, inspirational visual examples, and a variety of templates.

One of consultants I interviewed told me that it's no easy task to create workable guidelines that are universally useful. "The people executing the brand can be creative agencies who understand how to apply guidelines, or an administrative assistant creating a newsletter. If we write explanatory, how-to guidelines for the admin, creative agencies feel constrained. If we create multiple versions of guidelines to account for those less skilled, management needs to step in and guide them to the right person."

In this project, flexible brand assets proved too ambitious and time consuming. "We spent more than a year on a massive educational effort. We flew photographers around the world, created a single look, and wrote about how they should think about color, images, type, and so on. When we put it in the hands of local communicators, they spent six months trying to figure out what to do. When they started using the materials, they'd select the first example they liked and repeat it over and over."

When the branding agency returned to local sites for more user input, they found people paralyzed with options. "We then went the other way and developed an online library with templates for posters, brochures, everything they might need. By the time we got it all in place, a competitor launched a product that made the marketing message useless. Building the library just took too much time."

Where to implement this model

Centrally managed with flexibility may be best for larger companies with too many products and local variations to manage all creative demand from one location. For templates, the same principles from the centrally managed model apply: get input from users, make templates easy to work with, and train users in adapting them. Detailed guidelines have their place with creative vendors, but they're normally too much for average users.

Pitfalls and how to mitigate them

Risk: brand guidelines confuse users
In the example above, even marketing teams were overwhelmed with creative choices. Brand guidelines can be inspirational to skilled creative resources, but employee communications may not have those skills or the budget for working with vendors.

What to do about it: Offer practical workshops on the most frequently asked-for deliverables and walk users through applying brand standards. For greater and easier compliance with brand and style guidelines, tools like Acrolinx[2] offer solutions. Some may opt for an approach where machines are taught the rules and the application guides users toward the creation of guideline-compliant content. As artificial intelligence begins to creep into products, we can look forward to better tools to help us govern content production, assist users in crafting on-brand content, and prevent problems in source content that must be later translated and localized.

Risk: balancing brand consistency and local flexibility
When it comes to visual brand integrity, you get what you pay for. If you don't have enough affordable, skilled creative resources on hand, you'll see unauthorized variations. Offering business units a central creative services function is good, but it's not much help if those services are too expensive, if they insist on time-consuming brand reviews, or if they're quick to denounce local work as off brand without offering a solution.

What to do about it: If people can easily find options that are simple to use and that suit their purposes, they are less inclined to go out and create their own. Strike a balance. If you provide them with too many choices, it's easy to overwhelm them. Find out what users need most and provide it to them in useful formats. Continually train users on correct use. They will learn the guidelines more effectively with hands-on sessions.

---

[2] https://www.acrolinx.com/

Summary

Strengths:

- Richer creative potential
- More tailorable to local needs
- Greater local ownership

Weaknesses:

- More investment, both globally and locally
- Could be too much for local communicators
- May not be good for quickly changing industries
- Users need training, especially if you have many templates
- Needs more oversight on use of brand

Which organizations or business units it's best suited for:

- Business units willing to pay for creative support
- Stable environments where brand assets have a longer shelf life
- Countries with legally mandated local language requirements
- Larger business units with access to creative resources

Whose budget: As with the first model, creative resources are likely managed regionally or at Corporate, and costs for those services can be shared among business units. With guidelines, business units are free to engage local vendors or dedicate their own resources.

Autonomous teams with strong guidance

Centrally Managed		Autonomous Teams	
Limited Flexibility	Greater Flexibility	Strong Guidance	Minimal Guidance
← Greater central control — Greater autonomy →			

Co-creation is decentralized by definition, but it depends on dedicated, independent local teams with the tools, capabilities, and motivation to produce what the business needs. If the skills aren't there already, building them will be a long-term project. Trust is central to its working well.

Example: global consumer clothing company

A clothing company identified a set of youth subcultures that gravitated to its brand worldwide (skaters, rockers, surfers, etc.). They knew that each subculture had too much local variation for Corporate to engineer an effective approach everywhere, so they decided to develop resources locally who were familiar with the terrain. They identified teams, explained the purpose and mission, and gave them guidelines and templates. The local teams were encouraged to determine how to best express the company's identity in ways that would resonate with their target audience.

The company didn't attempt to understand these subcultures on their own. Instead, they hired people locally who were already part of them. The company developed a platform that was clear but unfinished, then gave each local community the freedom to build on it, without having to wait for approval.

Where to implement this model

Corporate articulates the intent and provides tools, but execution is entirely up to local teams. This model is suitable for companies whose services vary by location, or who have teams devoted to specific industry verticals (e.g., local teams focused on the auto industry in Germany but on textiles in Turkey). This approach may also be suitable for companies that deploy independent, unique-language social media teams.

Pitfalls and how to mitigate them

Risk: balancing purpose and autonomy

Communicators may start to identify more with the community they're serving than the company. New and unauthorized local channels could proliferate. At the same time, Corporate must check its impulse to edit or interfere because any sense of censorship could destroy credibility.

What to do about it: Provide advice and support. Offer frequent training and use the opportunity to build community among teams. Examining costs and budgets can be a good way to check progress. I spoke to one editorial manager with a creative agency that runs social media campaigns for the European Union. To balance creative freedom and oversight, he said that they provide social media teams in each country with a fixed, top-line budget. If a team burns through its budget more quickly than others, the agency helped them to make adjustments and prioritize work.

Summary

Strengths:

- Communications delivered with more authenticity
- Greater potential for audience engagement
- Empowers local teams

Weaknesses:

- Time consuming and potentially expensive

Which organizations or business units it's best suited for:

- Business units with unique targets, segments, market conditions
- Business units with experience in tailoring branded materials
- Business units with dedicated creative resources
- Startups and scale ups that commit to localization from the start

Whose budget : Probably corporate, but could be local, if business units see the value.

Autonomous teams with minimal guidance

Centrally Managed		Autonomous Teams	
Limited Flexibility	Greater Flexibility	Strong Guidance	Minimal Guidance
← Greater central control — Greater autonomy →			

Communicators in decentralized models must be continuously trained, and new people will take time to get up to speed. As your network's skills advance and as their experience deepens, they may want to assume more responsibility, eventually growing out of the centrally managed models and evolving toward processes that are more decentralized.

Example: a global technology brand establishes a newsroom

A conservatively managed global brand had long operated its communications function using a top-down messaging strategy. They rolled out a steady stream of products and updates, and messaging had to be constantly redefined. This centralized approach produced high-quality deliverables, but crafting them was time consuming and they were quickly out of date.

To re-structure their communications teams, they imitated what newspapers used to do with correspondents and news bureaus around the world. They installed experienced communicators in local markets who reported to a corporate newsroom. These local resources were responsible for executing local communications and making sure they conformed to the company's global character and purpose.

"Individual writers were embedded in the business units to support local executives in their routine reporting of week-to-week results and disconnects," said the consultant. "Most of these writers had journalism backgrounds, which is a mentality that understands context. They'd ask 'who are we talking to,' or 'is the strategy resonating,' and they reported upward on what they were hearing. If the executives or the writers saw opportunities to communicate something more intensively, they built a case for investing resources in it. In effect, they built an internal agency."

Where to implement this model

Autonomous teams with minimal guidance require more investment than other models, as well as more patience and trust. The people you put in place are not just skilled co-creators, they monitor local needs with a critical eye and deliver without having to ask permission or wait for support. They must be experienced and confident and know how to use communications to drive results. They should have the authority to stand up to local leaders when necessary, speak up about departures from strategy, make improvements, and deflect misguided requests.

Companies with extensive or complex offerings should think about this model, especially in markets that are of more strategic importance. Startups and scale ups with global ambitions should also consider it.

Pitfalls and how to mitigate them

Risk: retaining skilled communicators

Skilled people are hard to find, and replacing them when they leave takes more time. To effectively support the business, they have to become familiar with it, which also takes time.

What to do about it: Hire good people. Give them autonomy and freedom to act. Over time, invest in their professional development.

Risk: leaving them on their own for too long

Experienced communicators can function well on their own, so it's easy to forget about them. Yet no matter their seniority, people want to feel connected to a larger team of colleagues. If you don't provide that climate, they'll go work somewhere that does.

What to do about it: Autonomy is key, but so is connectedness and collaboration. To keep your team functioning well, you must help them maintain their skills and continually keep them in the discussion about how communications serves an evolving global strategy. The company must invest in them or they may leave, much sooner than you'd like.

Summary

Strengths:

- Enables more trust between Corporate and local businesses
- Prepares for crisis communications
- Results in higher quality local input

Weaknesses:

- Requires investment in a talent pipeline and maintenance of skills
- Replacing skilled resources can be time consuming

Which organizations or business units it's best suited for:

- Larger companies that can afford integrated communications teams in multiple markets
- Companies that are born global

Whose budget: Reporting lines are to Corporate, but costs can be allocated to local business units.

Putting the models together

Localization has variety at its core, and it isn't done the same way everywhere. If getting more local ownership of communications is worthwhile, decentralized communications may be the answer. But for some business units, communications that are executed locally can be too time intensive and provide too little pay off.

Moreover, no business stays the same forever. Markets evolve, conditions change, and budgets fluctuate. A merger, acquisition, or restructuring of the organization could change things overnight. With job mobility, your network capabilities are always going to be in flux.

As a result, some business units will modulate between models over time. When their needs or capabilities change, when they feel the practice is too expensive, or if their current model isn't working, they may move from central management to decentralized and then back again.

You must stay in tune with your network and what their business units need so that you can adjust the model for localization when necessary.

For example, suppose you lose a senior communicator in your biggest market where you operate an autonomous model with minimal guidance. You have to fill the role with an intern. In that case, it would be wise to move immediately to centrally managed with limited flexibility. If you discover later that the intern has visual or writing skills, you can then start planning for greater flexibility.

With an organization that's constantly in flux, it's best to have stable and reliable input for content that your whole network can draw from. Val Swisher recommends three core practices that she calls The Holy Trifecta.

> - **Use structured authoring:** Write once, use many.
> - **Manage terminology:** Say the same thing, the same way, every time you say it.
> - **Align translation memory:** Use already-translated terms in your source content. Manage them in source and translation.
>
> —Val Swisher, "The Holy Trifecta: Faster, Better, & Cheaper Global Content"[56]

She says that combining any of these (and optimally, all three) will get you better content in more languages for the least amount of time and money.

Localizing through a mix of these models and capabilities may need better tools than our traditional practices. In an upland Kapost blog post, Rahel Anne Bailie described marketing content operations that should sound familiar to internal communicators:

> "…a typical technology stack—and I use the word in a very tongue-in-cheek way—involves Google Docs or Microsoft Word, email for sign-offs, sticky notes on a computer monitor, and a spreadsheet to track it all. And we are so used to being system-poor and process-deficient that no one in our organizations is even recognizing the need for proper processes to be handled within a robust system to support content operations."
> —Rahel Anne Bailie, "Leveraging the Natural Connection Between ContentOps and Content Strategy"[3]

One thing that's important to understand is that no matter the model or the mix, there is always room for more local input. Fully empowering your network with flexible deliverables they can shape—to the extent that their skills and motivations allow—will give you better results.

A new world for templates

Managing and using templates may be more affordable and flexible thanks to subscription services such as Beautiful.AI[3] and Prezi.[4] Beautiful.AI allows subscribers to create, store and share templates in the cloud so that people who need slide decks can access templates that are approved and up-to-date. Beautiful.AI templates allow universal changes in style, so that users can adapt slides to be appropriate for a new audience with slightly different visual needs. Prezi offers similar, cloud-based capabilities.

While services like these were designed for people outside the design world, success often depends on user training. No matter what tools or techniques you use, training can help drive adoption, alleviate the traditional headaches of managing multiple versions, and greatly improve the visual quality of local deliverables. To drive adoption beyond the communications department and further into the organization, consider using interactive product walkthroughs.[5]

---

[3] https://www.beautiful.ai/
[4] https://prezi.com/
[5] This Whatfix blog post shows some examples: "Why Multi Billion-dollar Enterprises Are Adopting Interactive Walkthroughs in 2019"[50].

Part II Conclusion

Conventional corporate communications practice is to create and send, and for many practitioners, that's the only thing they can imagine. Other business stakeholders can be limited in their thinking as well. As it is, they rarely understand what Communications can do for them and what input and timelines are needed to be effective.

The transition to localization and higher-level co-creation is a significant change. Everyone is going to have to learn how it works: leadership at corporate, local leaders in markets of every size, managers of global functions—and communicators themselves.

To realize the potential of localization, you need to have realistic planning, the ability to articulate the benefits to and responsibilities of stakeholders, and clarity on the approach, governance, goals, and milestones.

Low- and No-Cost Strategies

It seems that Corporate Communications has more to gain from business units than the other way around. Global organizations like telling the world how global they are, and to prove it, they look for content originating from beyond the headquarters' home country to share in social media and in reports on *corporate social responsibility (CSR)*.

We need to flip that script. In this part, I look at simple practices that can make corporate output more helpful and local output more likely to resonate. You can start small, but you must start.

What You'll Learn: Simple steps that enable localization without investing heavily.

Why You Should Care: Without increasing your budget, your work can have impact on international outcomes.

CHAPTER 8
Preparing for Localization

We must stop producing campaigns that end with scripted, awkward launches as depicted in Figure 2.3 (p. 29).

You could prevent such disappointments if you could orchestrate events so expertly that they would be received favorably everywhere. That is unlikely, if not impossible. If you must do global campaigns, make them flexible, so they can be re-purposed locally for more impact.

The Cinderella story has many variations. The Brothers Grimm had stepsisters chopping off toes to get into the shoe, another version had wish-granting acorns, and Disney added singing mice. Despite those differences, we recognize the story: a prince falls for a poor woman, she goes missing but leaves a shoe, and, in the end, they're happily united.

As long as the principal message gets through, the small differences don't matter. As Carmen Simon's work suggests, messages with cultural reinforcers are more likely to be memorable and acted on. Your local team is in the best position to give your message cultural references that work for their staff.

"People always intend to do something next," Carmen Simon writes in *Impossible to Ignore*[48]. "It is more likely they will pay attention to cues linked to *their* intentions versus *your* intentions. Connecting the proper cues to the proper intentions is the first entry point toward influencing others' memory and actions." (emphasis is mine)

With a good process for localization and co-creation, corporate provides basic direction, and business units do the legwork. A well-executed communication combines company strategy and local proof points to make it memorable.

In an interview, Simon told me there is "always an opportunity to link content to what the brain finds reflexive." That's why instead of creating centrally and selectively translating, you should enable locations to formulate content on their own—content that's relevant, memorable, high quality, and on brand.

If you want local markets to support the brand and company mission, you have to learn to trust each other. Communicators in the countries, the regions, and the head office must closely examine their roles and areas of expertise and decide where they can best contribute. And while local people may feel as though they've brought it up countless times, they must be tireless and continually point out what's not working and what they need to fix it.

What headquarters and local businesses can learn from each other

The reputation of the Ivory Tower is well earned, but despite what some local people think, people at headquarters can contribute. Communicators at corporate are often more specialized and experienced, and they can share their lessons and best practices with local content creators, teaching them how to weave in strategy, improve visuals, and measure business impact. They can also advise on when to consider storytelling and an emotional appeal and why those techniques can get better results. Corporate should also help with planning content calendars because—ideally—they know what's coming from the global message machine.

Regions and local business units have a responsibility to keep corporate informed about audience needs and resource constraints. When managers at corporate refuse to act on this information time after time, it can be frustrating and discouraging. Local people working on communications can easily come to see corporate as unified and unresponsive.

Corporate communicators must understand that local business models, culture, and tools differ. Because responsibilities and resources at headquarters constantly shift, educating people in the Ivory Tower takes continuous effort. Local communicators should remind corporate of these differences at every opportunity, even if it makes them feel like nags.

If corporate must roll out a global campaign, they should find ways to facilitate local adaptations. If the organization can't be persuaded to take that time, and you know that local input was minimal or nonexistent during preparation, look for supplemental tactics that would give the campaign more relevance, such as creating unique local content along the same themes.

Regions and business units must become strategic partners with Communications; corporate needs to learn what's useful and interesting to regions and business units. Both sides must be willing to learn, and that requires trust that's earned over time.

> Practical Tip: Tomorrow is relative: Beware of time references
>
> If you're creating an announcement for internal channels, avoid time references that are immediately inaccurate. If you announce at 3:00 PM in New York that "Today is earnings day," it's already past the close of business in Europe and Asia. Better to use something more universally accurate, such as: "Earnings released on (specific calendar date)." A message with a time reference should be true no matter when people see it.

The role of local business units in localization

Most of my career has been spent in support of corporate headquarters. My biggest advice for local communications is this: don't wait for perfect, because it's not coming.

> The solution isn't to mandate that all content come from headquarters. That won't work. You can't get customized content to each region, specifically targeted to a local culture, properly localized, translated, or transcreated in time to meet every region's needs. You can strategize and plan all you like, but it won't work. No one knows a region as well as the people who live there. The solution is to reach out to all your locations and involve them in the plan.
>
> —Val Swisher, *Global Content Strategy*[54]

I wrote the section below to give local communicators a sense of what they can expect from their region and global counterparts and to suggest how local communicators can play a part in transforming global content and enabling locally relevant communications.

Be an active participant

Years of top-down communication methods have convinced corporate that local employees wait patiently for its decisions and announcements. Yet that arrogance and self-satisfaction isn't the only problem with conventional practices. Corporate's incuriosity about local realities, combined with their desire to maintain control, has instilled passivity and bad practices in local business units.

Don't wait for fully formed corporate deliverables that will work perfectly in your location. On its own, the corporate office will never figure out the needs of your business. Even if you've brought up issues in the past that weren't acted on, bring them up again. Leadership, approaches, and function heads are always changing at the corporate office, so even if you've lobbied for something in the past and were ignored, bring it up again.

Don't settle for English if you think localized versions will help. If you don't demand it, corporate will continue to be bewildered when people don't engage with their campaigns. Eventually, they'll hear you when you tell them that language and culture matter.

Corporate also routinely forgets to explain the purpose of its deliverables. Some will say the campaign is to "drive engagement," but that's not specific enough. Insist on background and context for global campaigns. You weren't at the meeting when the CEO made the demand, so it's reasonable to ask about purpose. Corporate always believes their campaigns are urgent, so on briefing calls, be sure to ask why. What problems does it solve, and how will success be measured? They should know.

Act autonomously

Your company culture may demand compliance and cascades, but it's time for you to recognize that you are the local communicator. Take the lead. It may never be assigned to you.

Don't expect too much from corporate. If you meekly ask them to approve local content, they may not even reply. Like everyone, they're often overwhelmed with increasing demands, and they don't want to assume decision-making responsibility for your market too.

Of course, feel free to ask their opinion on tactics. They'll be happy to advise you (especially regarding measurement of impact). But if you ask for permission to deliver a message in a particular manner—face to face, in a town hall, or in team meetings—or if you ask for permission to reinforce a message with posters or a social campaign, you may not get a thoughtful answer. Decisions are intimidating, and from a corporate perspective, many of them should be up to you. You know your culture and business needs better than they do. Go for it.

Continually make your demands known

Business units occasionally ask corporate to review their work for brand compliance. Almost always, the answer is that it's not up to standard, which gives business units no incentive to ask for brand reviews in the future.

You're within your rights to complain if creative support for graphics, video or other visual media is hard to come by. To be fair to my brand colleagues, they're forced to prioritize how they spend their time—usually through an internal chargeback of costs. That chargeback is designed so that if some groups consistently take more of their time than their profitability should allow, the company can make adjustments.

But that won't help you in the short term. If your work has been deemed off brand and you've given corporate plenty of lead time, demand support. Disapproval by itself is not enough. Reviewers need to make corrections or clearly demonstrate how you can bring the content into compliance with the tools available to you. If the answer is that your content is forbidden and corporate won't offer an affordable solution, you need to push for a solution that's practical and long-term.

You may not be able to visually localize communications right away, but unless you continue to push for adequate resources, the budget you need will never be allocated to your business unit.

Use corporate as a resource

While you should take the lead, you don't need to work in isolation. Corporate can—and should—provide assistance, such as the following:

- A sounding board for ideas that you want to execute
- A source for advice on best practices
- A creative resource for executing more visually advanced deliverables such as graphics and video
- An ally for convincing your local leadership that investing in communications pays off
- A mentor for developing your career in communications

Corporate communicators are likely on top of industry trends, and they've fought internal battles for resources many times. They know what arguments have worked in the past, and they'll be happy to know that you share an interest with them.

Build communications skills, boost your career

Localization is going to require more from you, and creating and adapting communications develops skills on several levels. Even if your efforts are modest, taking the responsibility for actively shaping communications will teach you things that will serve you throughout your career.

You will also be doing your part to drive business outcomes. Because you're directly involved, you can track results and connect them to your efforts. Measure before and after, and get the results into your résumé.

Take ownership

In the end, you and your leadership are the local communicators. Most of the time, corporate will not—in fact cannot—solve your communication problems. But with your guidance, leaders can deliver things differently, begin allocating resources, and provide more input. You must decide what your team needs to achieve and what will help deliver the best results. When you take ownership your responsibilities and workload will increase, but the rewards will be to your credit.

Localization 101: budgeting time for in-country review

Those outside of employee communications see the function as entirely reactive, putting out one-off announcements as needed. There's a fair amount of that, thanks to traditional mindsets, unforeseen circumstances, and leaders who want what they want.

However, the planned output of employee communications isn't that different from sales and marketing: simultaneous, multiple initiatives supporting a range of business objectives, with schedules and measurable goals.

When it comes to planned output, the most important factor to help make content compelling to employees is longer timelines. If you aim an initiative at employees outside your home market, you need to extend production timelines and involve countries in your planning and execution.

> Extending global rollout dates to allow for in-country review and revision is the best investment you can make in employee localization.

Reviews save costs because they can prevent big, embarrassing mistakes. In-country review has never been more necessary. As *machine translation* is applied to more content and more channels, you need a process for local review to help prevent embarrassing errors and user frustration.

Let's face it—no two facilities are exactly alike, let alone entire markets. Products and services vary by locale, depending on factors such as the degree of automation, the extent of outsourcing, local regulations, and client segments. Every local landscape is unique, so even translated global content can be problematic.

In-country reviews should take place well before you share corporate-created deliverables with employees, and they should always be included in project rollout plans. This takes more time than just releasing a deliverable and seeing what happens, but the additional time you allot to this portion of the content cycle will contribute positively to the final product.

It's also a good idea to have additional reviewers from outside marketing or Communications. Reconciling review input takes time, and it can be tough to distinguish changes that are essential from those that are just one person's stylistic opinion, but despite those challenges, collaboration will give the content more significance and credibility.

The importance of taking time

I got my start in communications before our work was called *content*. Back then, initiatives and announcements were coordinated and timed to hit all markets simultaneously, usually just as the press release was issued. A hurry-up, 24/7 global organization no longer expects to deploy all messaging to all points on the globe simultaneously, but old mindsets are still common. Once you accept that simultaneity isn't always necessary, take the next step and help international locations make the best of this newer flexibility.

Don't make reviews an urgent request. Reviews should be meaningful and substantive. Allow adequate time for planning and execution, and make sure your local network gets enough time.

The corollary—corporate review of local deliverables—is also valuable. If your localization program is just starting out, you should budget time to review local work for *brand identity* compliance, message distortion, and departure from company strategy. But look at this as a qualitative check, not a measure of translation accuracy. The local team made their wording choices for a reason. Don't demand a strict translation of your original.

Corporate stands to learn useful lessons from such reviews. Rosie Halfhead told me that corporate reviews of local content helped her team at headquarters understand how to improve the usefulness of their work. "It was particularly valuable for the global team, as they learned and understood more about local differences and context."

In the long term, sheer volume makes reviewing every local version unrealistic, but once you establish greater trust, you can reduce corporate reviews. Corporate and the network should be doing triage to determine what needs review and what doesn't. Otherwise, corporate will waste time reviewing babies and birthdays, leaving business units on their own to explain strategy.

Where English can be effective

Each time you produce something for global distribution, Communications and the business units should weigh the need to translate, localize, or co-create. You must thoroughly assess the need, side by side with your network. Some business units will agree that English is the best language for them. And English-only can work in certain operational and informational instances, such as the following:

- Routine updates presented in a well-known format (e.g., delivered in a template)
- Notifications for management on operational topics or incidents
- Login instructions for an application that's used only occasionally
- Unexpected announcements that must be disseminated fast
- Material information that must be made available in the same format everywhere

These examples are informational, and that's where English can have the most reach. But when you are using English, it's best to use plain language. For instructions, provide visuals (or at least screen shots) to help users. When you need to persuade, use local language, even if just for portions of your message.

Inform in English, persuade in local language

A message entirely in local language commands more attention. But you probably can't afford to translate or localize every internal communication, so you must prioritize. In assessing these priorities, don't be distracted by the importance of the message in its entirety (most messengers will claim theirs is of the highest importance). Instead, think about the purpose of each component of the message. A blend of English and local language might have more success.

The examples in the previous section—where notifications in English may be acceptable—are largely informational. If your organization functions reasonably well in English, then most users can manage to interpret information presented in it.

Yet inspiring people to care about that information is where most corporate communications fail. It's not that users don't understand the message, it's that they don't care enough to take time to decipher it. When you're trying to persuade someone to take notice or to change behavior, local language makes a big difference. In these parts of your message, it's best to shift to the local language.

Example: sorting information from persuasion

A group that processes expense reimbursements wants your help. They tell you that people aren't submitting expense reports correctly, and they ask you to push out an announcement. Since it's a pain point for them, they believe it's urgent, and they want an email message sent out to everyone right away. They say they don't have time or budget to translate.

Getting to the business need behind a request like this is a classic internal communications exercise. In this case, you need to help the group understand the difference between important and urgent.[1] They must also understand that they have to pinpoint their audience. Sending a message to all employees is lazy because not everyone submits expense reports. They must investigate the problem a little more deeply and find out where the mistakes are happening, what kind of user is committing them, how the mistakes can best be prevented, and so on.

In administrative matters like this, your message typically needs to remind people of the correct procedure, or teach them something that wasn't clear in the first place. If some of the offenders are outside the English-speaking world, you need to decide whether to translate the message. If it's exclusive to management, as a request like this one probably is, you might decide that a single email to managers in plain language is enough. But if email is poorly read and acted on in your organization,[2] the problem may persist, and you will need to deal with it later on. (There are often better choices than email, but hear me out with this example).

---

[1] One good introduction to coaching people through this is "Guiding Non-Comms Colleagues Through Internal Comms Challenges"[2] from Alive With Ideas.

[2] "The Benchmark of Successful Internal Email Campaigns"[23] from hppy provides benchmarks in open and click rates for internal emails by industry, courtesy of Newsweaver (now Poppulo).

The expense report tool is probably in English, and while that may be a root cause to the problem, changes to that tool are probably more than this group has patience or budget for.

But localizing an email—in whole or in part—is more achievable. Konstantin Dranch, language industry researcher, told me that he once experimented with local language subject lines for marketing email sent to people in the US, Europe, and Asia. The body of the message was all in English, but when he localized the subject lines, he saw a thirty percent increase in open rates. A similar tactic may work well with internal email as well.

The message portion itself can also be partially localized. An email message about the expense report tool probably follows a predictable structure. The first part of the message explains the problem with enough context for users to know what's in it for them. The second part tells users what action they need to take.

In this example, the portions of your communication that are meant to inspire people to care and to take action should be localized. Once you've got the audience's attention and persuaded them that it's worth doing correctly, you can use English in the part of the message that informs them of the steps they need to take. You might even be able to deploy machine translations for these informational portions.

> If there's no time to translate the entire communication, provide the introductory, motivational portion in local language. The informational portion may be acceptable in plain-language English.

Your network can help you determine what will motivate your target audience to take action. And they can help craft and localize the motivational portion of the message.

Targeted campaign briefings

Communications often briefs messengers and local management to help them prepare content for delivery and show them how to distribute and re-purpose it. If you're not already creating such briefings and providing delivery and guidance for re-use, you should start.

To make briefings effective, they should be targeted. Consider the background and aspirations of each recipient. Refer to the market types from Chapter 5 to make your briefings specific for each type of messenger.

In countries where admins or specialist-level employees from other functions carry out your plans (that is, they're only partially dedicated to you), provide short and precise instructions in plain language. In countries where the staff has more skills and time, you can give them recommendations appropriate to their level of commitment, knowledge, and experience. In large markets that have skilled resources in place, provide additional background on the project, such as its goals and how you'll measure success.

> A one-size-fits-all brief will either be condescending or overly complicated. It limits the potential of those more dedicated to communications and intimidates those without much experience.

At first you may not know much about the members of your network, but the more you work together, the more you will learn about what they can and can't do. One-on-one interaction is best to find out more about each network member's personality and what motivates them to help.

Is it a formal part of their role or is it a favor? What have they worked on in the past? Are they studying communications practices on their own time? Is communications a field they want to support?

It could be that their career aspirations have nothing to do with internal communication. On the other hand, maybe a place on that career path was just the break they were looking for. You may discover someone from another department who just finished a marketing or communications degree, or someone who maintains a good blog. You may have to do some political wrangling to be allowed to develop a person who doesn't directly report to you, but for the right person, fostering a feeling of inclusion could pay off in the long run.

As with all communications deliverables, the more you know about your audience the better. Reach out to your local messengers and include them in the planning as early as possible.

CHAPTER 9
Managing Translation

My ideal communication system looks more like co-creation than the traditional announce-and-translate, but for most companies, getting to that ideal will take time. In the first stages of localizing communications, the success of many initiatives will hinge on how well you manage content in multiple languages.

Learn when and how your company translates

If your company has a translation process and preferred vendors, that process was built for content targeted to customers, not employees. Therefore, externally focused communicators are probably more familiar with translation timelines, vendors, and budgets.

For internal communications, translation is more often the responsibility of local business units. Like corporate, they don't want to allocate budget to translation, so to save money, someone in the office does it.

> Local businesses may not know exactly how much professional translation costs, but they don't share corporate's view that having local employees translate campaigns is free.

Local staff spend hours on translations, and the same person may be expected to translate content from other global departments as well. In short, you may not realize how much time local staff spend translating content, and the fact that you don't know breeds resentment when the workload gets high.

You must determine how much translation local business units are doing and whether the people doing it are part of the internal communications network. An informal audit of how much time and money business units spend on translation is the first step toward finding opportunities for translation efficiency.

Back at corporate, get familiar with how the various parts of your company manage translations today. Knowing how sales, marketing, and public relations decide what should be translated, what processes they follow, and what vendors they use will inform you as you build a localization program. You may uncover relatively easy opportunities to re-purpose content, and you might also find ways to leverage existing tools, workflow, and resources.

The dangers of skimping on translation

Skimping on translation for content is like buying cheap curtains for a mansion. As John Yunker wrote in *Think Outside the Country*[63], "What I often ask companies before we begin talking about translation costs is to first put a price on the creation of all of the source language content, which is usually in English. It's important to understand what you've invested on your primary website, as well as apps and collateral materials, to place the costs of any localization efforts in better context." Nevertheless, he concedes that "It's not hard to exceed a million dollars in translation costs to support 20 languages."

To keep the final invoice as low as possible, avoid last-minute rush jobs and make certain that other departments understand international needs and timelines. Make sure project managers at headquarters understand the necessity of translation and localization and plan appropriate timelines.

Make the cost of translation a staple in your year-over-year budget, or better yet, get it into the budgets of internal stakeholders so the task is no longer a surprise in project plans.

Assessing and prioritizing costs for translations

Employee communication budgets usually can't afford translations for all markets, so they must select the languages that have the most impact.

When you provide translated content for the first time, the initial response from the local office may not be enthusiastic. If you ask someone to assess translation quality, know that their opinion will be subjective. If somebody tells you that a translation is bad, they may be right, but they may also not like the subject matter. Before you condemn a translation as substandard, consider the source of the assessment and their reasoning, and then validate their assessment with others.

Cultural background can influence their assessment. I've heard people from France assert that Québécois is not French. I'm told the differences between Spanish in Spain versus Spanish in Latin America are significant. Depending on who you've worked with in the UK, you may have heard withering dismissals of American English. As a New Worlder I find these preferences unfair, but my opinion isn't important. It's bad business to spend time and money on translations that annoy and alienate those you are trying to reach, convince, and convert.

To make sure the quality of your translations remains high, ask your network to monitor the content they're getting and let you know what they think of it. If there is a problem, discuss with them how to address it. It may be an unskilled translator, but it could also be something internal to your organization, such as the following:

- Translators get content too late to do a good job.
- Translators are unfamiliar with the business unit that produced the original content.
- The original content is badly written.
- In-country reviewers are not looking closely enough.

Many things can go wrong in this process. If you can pinpoint the problem together, you can jointly decide what actions to take. It may not be realistic for you to examine each deliverable in depth, but a regular assessment of both source content and the resulting translations is a good first step toward creating high-quality content.

> **Practical Tip**
>
> Headquarters in the US are lucky when it comes to doing business in the UK, since we Anglophones (kind of) understand each other. But it would be wise to start treating the Queen's English as a distinct language. There are significant differences in syntax, spelling, usage, and culture, and US-generated English content doesn't feel local to UK audiences. Just as you would for France, schedule time and budget for in-country review.

What languages do you need?

Headcount is the most common criteria used to allocate translation budget for employee content. If your desired outcome hinges on sheer numbers, you translate for the largest language groups until you run out of money. With just a few languages, many companies can reach more than 80 percent of their employees.

But your company might benefit from a more sophisticated allocation for translations. Yunker advises marketers, "Your language portfolio should reflect your global growth strategy"[63]. When translating global corporate deliverables for employees, or when assessing which countries would benefit most from localization, consider a wider range of criteria in your decision.

Targeting key languages

Translation costs for each language are not the same, and per/word rates often correlate with the country's cost of labor. Scandinavian languages are said to be the most expensive, while the cheapest are in Southeast Asia. Which languages you include in your translation set can significantly affect your overall budget.

You should also assess which languages don't get a translation. Since a small set of languages normally covers a majority of employees, companies get into a routine and translate only for the same, fixed set of language groups. They leave small languages out, maybe forever. Employees in countries like Slovenia, Hungary, or Denmark may never see corporate content in their native language, which means their relationship with corporate content will always be distant and alien.

Budgets limit what we translate, but it's also an opportunity to perform some detailed cost/benefit analysis. The beauty of smaller countries is that you can test several approaches and see which give you better results.

For example, translating English content into German may be too expensive for a specific project, while the costs for Polish and Romanian could be within reach. Neither may be major markets for your company, but translating content in more affordable markets gives you an opportunity to evaluate in detail the return on investment for translation and localization. You can extrapolate the results to other markets.

Other factors to consider in allocating translation budget

If your goal is to push people to complete training and global compliance, you may want to focus translations on countries where participation is historically low. It may be better to spend your funds on countries with the lowest levels of English proficiency, the lowest levels of engagement with corporate content, or the lowest levels of compliance with similar initiatives in the past.

If you want to know whether translation can boost engagement with global content generally, a few digital deliverables translated for countries where your employees are demographically younger could provide data to inform your broader content strategy. For example, companies looking to recruit among younger, tech-savvy candidates across multiple countries might consider a ranking of the language groups most commonly used by game developers[17].

Targeting translations to achieve a specific local goal can help you evaluate success, and it brings local countries into the process. Just a few deliverables in select countries that normally wouldn't see corporate translations helps you build alliances with local functions and future localizers.

Another factor to consider in allocating translation budget is total user experience. Instead of translating entire channels or initiatives, think about critical processes. In an article in *Multilingual*, John Yunker advises international marketers to consider what he calls scenario-based localization, translating content that supports desired outcomes such as lead generation, direct sales online, or indirect sales through partners.[1]

Internal communicators can think about focusing their translation budget on similarly unified processes, such as expense reporting, compulsory training, or internal recruiting. Is the entire click-through of a process presented in the local language, or does it start users down the path only to leave the final steps in English? Narrowing in on these is an opportunity to work closely with local businesses and keep both sides focused on outcomes instead of output. "A scenario-based approach focuses your global and local teams on ensuring that the local websites have true value for end users…"[64].

In short, calibrate your translation choices with business needs and align them with the purpose of your content. As always, involve local people in the decision. Experiments like these add complexity to the process, but mixing up your translation set is a great opportunity to measure and assess.

Localizing interfaces

For many internal tools, navigational elements—the fill-in-the-blank fields for personal data or next-step clicks like **continue** and **submit**—are in English. This is especially true for interfaces in tools for once-a-year tasks like compulsory training on anti-corruption compliance. Communications and human resources often have to ask users repeatedly to complete this type of training, so anything that increases awareness, acceptance and participation would be welcome.

Localizing the tool itself would boost participation, but there may not be time or money for that. In those cases, you have three choices:

1. Do nothing and hope for the best. Expect more time and energy spent on chasing people to complete the training.
2. Create supplemental instructions in the local language using screen shots to show navigation. Arlene Birt told me that these workarounds are evidence of inadequate user analysis.

---

[1] "What the best global websites have in common"[64].

3. Make use of Daniel Foster's Simplified User Interface, a graphical alternative to screen shots.[2] By creating simple, instructional, animated videos and voicing them or subtitling them in local language, user instructions can be more effective and less expensive than localizing the entire tool.

Resource considerations

For internal translations, the next critical factor is whether you have people who can translate, review, or localize. Because of employee turnover, these capabilities are always evolving. Just because a business unit translates today doesn't mean it will forever. When budgets are under pressure, a local business may retreat to English if it sees the time and costs as extravagant.

One Belgium-based director of communications and learning and development at the regional head office of a global healthcare company told me that in 2016, her company was questioning for a second time whether content in multiple languages was delivering enough return. Belgium has three official languages.

"We simply didn't have that luxury anymore, both in terms of people and money. Our medical terminology required double- or triple-checking translations, which took valuable time. Doing this for a handful of people in a handful of countries just didn't make sense anymore."

Her team decided to re-try machine translation, and they anticipated resistance because when they'd tried it ten years earlier, employees widely complained. In their second attempt, people were more accepting.

Audience and medium

When that same company wanted the attention of salespeople however, the director admitted that they invested in human delivery of local language. "At our annual sales conference we outlined the objectives and strategy for the year, and we did live interpretation. It's essential that people get those messages loud and clear."

---

[2] "The Value of Visual Content and a Simplified User Interface"[20].

I found this surprising, because I had always assumed in-person *interpreting* was significantly more expensive than written translations. But when it comes to media, there is a range of localizing options, and you shouldn't assume costs will be out of reach without first consulting a language services provider. Depending on what you're trying to achieve and who you're trying to reach, there may be options you hadn't thought of.

For example, Mark Ohlsen told me that the cost of video localization depends on the purpose, length, and language set. Live translation at an event may be cheaper than translating follow-up documents, especially if the audience—like most sales forces—won't read them. For panel discussions or instructional content that need precision, he said that recording the content and later adding voice-overs or subtitles can be more cost effective. Assuming that live interpreters are rock-star expensive—as I did—is a mistake. To understand your options, you must ask.

Mixing translation and localization

Your company's strategic markets—larger countries or places with greater opportunities for growth—are probably at the top of your list for translations. Smaller language groups may never be part of your equation.

But that doesn't mean anyone needs to be left out. Where you have budget for translations, establish in-country review. Where you have skilled resources, enable co-creation. For smaller markets with less investment, provide easy-to-use visual templates they can adapt. Involve local people, set up meaningful tests, and measure the results. If those results prove positive in high-priority areas, you may get budget sooner than you think.

> **Practical Tip: Occasional love for the small countries**
> Employees in smaller markets often say that they're resigned to content that's not in their language. Passing through their cities and watching their TV, it's true that a lot of the commercial landscape is in English. At the same time, it's hard to imagine that corporate content outside their language is delightful. An occasional translation might go a long way toward building some rapport. Combined with some finely tuned measurement, it gives you test cases to learn from.

Why you need plain language

In the preface, I wrote about a branding project where my team's clever writing did a disservice to a pan-European project. The content we had worked so hard to create was too smart for its own good, and the translators and copywriters found it had too much wordplay to be useful.

According to Val Swisher, that experience isn't unusual.

> "What you should not do is take your new, witty, hip branding and assume that you can translate it into Farsi, Arabic, Mandarin, or any other language without evaluating it—the language, the images, the layout, the medium, and everything about it—for cultural appropriateness. You might end up creating one of those disasters that people like me write about."
> —Val Swisher, *Global Content Strategy*[54]

In my re-branding project, we should have spent less time perfecting our English content in isolation and more time discussing intent with staff writers in other languages. While our content was a fine start, we should have taken an additional step and given them not just our creative original, but also a summary of each content block's objective and a version in plain English, stripped of idioms and puns. That would have given our colleagues a chance to co-create.

> Good writing is refined so that it's human, simple, and conversational. But it can also be idiomatic and cultural. If you have polished native-language content, you should consider it a single, local-market version. Then work backwards and create a new original in plain language to share with translators and localizers.

Accessible buildings aren't just for the disabled. They're for children, the elderly, the injured, the distracted, and people struggling with bags of groceries. Likewise, accessible, plain language is good for everybody. It improves the accuracy of output from automated translation tools, it makes translations of all kinds easier and cheaper, and it makes content more accessible. For broader communication, plain language versions get localizers and co-creators closer to deploying effective content across multiple markets.

> **Practical Tip: E1 and E2**
>
> In English-teaching circles, E1 is shorthand for native English speakers, while E2 describes those who learned it as a foreign language. Producers of global content should always keep the distinction in mind and know whether they're working on content for E1 or E2.

Idiomatic vs. plain language

We're often told that jokes and puns don't translate, but given people's abilities in English and awareness of pop culture, I'm sometimes tempted to ignore this advice. I tend to fall for clever headlines, but when I check my ego, I realize I have to let these go for international versions. If you've suffered someone telling you a joke translated from his native language word-for-word, you'll understand why.

Headlines are easy to change, but you've got problems if a playful style continues throughout the piece.

> If humor is central to your message, budget time for localization, not translation.

Jokes aren't the only references that don't travel. Native speakers write with idioms, metaphors, and cultural references that people in their geography understand. These culturally specific references slip in unconsciously, and you need to be constantly looking for and avoiding them.[3]

If you have creative copy—content that's colorful to you and reads smoothly—use it in your own market. I call this content *Jazz Hands*. Content in plain language without cultural references I call *Just the Facts*.

Early drafts of this book were written in my best Jazz Hands because I wanted to persuade companies, especially in my native US, that localization of English-language content is both needed and achievable. Fortunately for you, my editors convinced me to simplify.

---

[3] For more on this topic, see Barbara Gibson's *Intercultural competencies needed by global CEOs.*[21] and Chapter 12.

If you haven't already sensed it, Just the Facts is less creatively satisfying to writers' egos, but it may be preferable to most readers. "Tell people what they need to know, not what you want to tell them," said Deborah S. Bosley. "We are all too busy to read any more than is absolutely necessary to answer our questions, take action, or understand the content."

My own relationship with purple prose is contradictory: I can't stand it in others, but I tend to indulge it in my own writing. It's a lifelong battle. If Jazz Hands has any magic at all, it's to capture attention and possibly to persuade. Leave that for advertising. Just the Facts is more valuable in almost everything else we work on.

One last reason why plain language will get you better results. For global readers, it's more engaging. I live in Prague, and my Czech is good, but not great. I miss a lot. But if a tour guide speaks Czech in a way that I can understand, or I pick up a magazine and I feel like I'm getting the point in most articles, I get excited. And I buy more issues of that magazine.

The sober accuracy of Just the Facts will be easier for everyone involved in localization, and the final product doesn't have to be dull. If you set up an effective localization and co-creation process, markets will incorporate cultural references if they need to, creating their own Jazz Hands content that readers will respond to.

Providing machine translations

When it comes to working with other languages, life has never been easier. At work, I use Google Translate to get a quick impression of content outside my language, and in my personal life it's a huge time saver with messages from my bank or power company. The translations aren't artfully rendered, but I normally get the gist (most of these important-looking letters turn out to be spam).

People debate whether we'll ever be able to rely entirely on machine translations, but it's clear they're here to stay. Translation companies have been using automated tools for years to lower costs and turn work around faster.

And for end users like me, these tools help us understand content that gets pushed at us, especially if it's longer and more technical.

For content that corporate functions create and distribute, the use of machine translation is a different story. When corporate uses machine translation for content, the audience howls.

To be honest, I don't fully appreciate why. I understand that some languages get better results than others, but even for languages that translate more intelligibly, even when we offer a disclaimer that it's an automated translation, they still howl.

While machine translation is going to be an increasingly important and usable tool, you shouldn't expect it to solve your international communication problems on its own.

Machine translations are becoming increasingly useful for low-risk, matter-of-fact, clearly written instructions. They're also being implemented in line-level tools that corporate communications doesn't control or have awareness of, so a clear process for in-country, in-language review of content has never been more important.

When offering machine translation, user opt-in is the best choice. Employees who complain about the quality of machine translations add that we should also let them have access to the English original. That seems fair enough. Functionality that presents both the original and the automatically translated content side-by-side, under user control, gives them choice and reduces time spent.

It may be years—if ever—before automated translation is effective with creative, emotional content, but tolerance for it and its shortcomings is likely to grow as translation technology gets better.

When presenting English-language content to non-native speakers, these are your options, ranked by user preference:

- High-quality and professionally translated
- Automatically translated and labeled as such, with the English original readily available
- English only
- Automatically translated with no source content available

Using style guides for better translations

Style guides document an organization's conventions for spelling, usage, terminology, and more. They're created to help writers create consistent content that communicates effectively.

The Associated Press (AP) Stylebook[4] was originally created for US journalists, and global companies often use it as a foundation, supplementing it with company-specific terms.

I started my career as a writer, so I love style guides. They're handy rulebooks that I can turn to for answers, and they serve as a judge for disputes (e.g., "Should we use the '%' symbol or spell it out as 'percent'?"). I learn something every time I read one, which I do thanks to a writing teacher who told me to re-read a style guide once a year. It's good advice.

Style guides represent the collective will of the organization. Or more accurately, the collective will of the communications department.

Some clients have trouble locating their current style guide, which leads me to believe that no one has consulted it in years. These printed or pdf style guides just don't seem to be a serious way to enforce style, even if I personally empathize with their authors.

> No matter how long or short, style guides are generally ignored by everyone except those in Communications.

---

[4] https://www.apstylebook.com/

This gap in official style versus what people actually do could change, thanks to technologies such as Qordoba,[5] VisibleThread,[6] and Acrolinx,[7] which make content style easier to govern. Acrolinx can be programmed to guide authors as they write, and cloud-based Frontify[8] claims to help improve brand consistency by sharing guidelines online with all who need them. These tools could provide at least a first step in ensuring everyone has access to, and uses, the same rules.

Even if your organization can't afford tools like these, one guide I recommend for centrally created content for international business units is John Kohl's *The Global English Style Guide: Writing Clear, Translatable Documentation for a Global Market*[28]. It's a finely detailed and well-organized reference work for writers preparing content for translation. It details grammatical structures that are problematic not just for automated translation software, but also for non-native speakers and translators.

Although written with procedures and technical documentation in mind, Kohl's guide is useful in any context using machine translation because it makes the output more accurate and less annoying to users. While traditional style guides are devoted to spelling and punctuation, *Global English* looks more closely at sentence structure to show writers how to optimize their content for global consumption.

The book's examples demonstrate how simpler sentences remove ambiguity and make text easier to understand. "It's not an issue of word count, it's an issue of grammatical complexity," said Kohl in our interview. "If a sentence has more than two clauses, it's not as likely to come out as well as a less complex sentence. Even if a sentence sounds perfectly fine, there may be complexity that software can't handle. A short, 17-word sentence in three clauses might come out of translation software as garbage, whereas if you divided it into three small sentences, it would come out fine."

---

[5] https://qordoba.com/
[6] https://www.visiblethread.com/
[7] https://www.acrolinx.com/
[8] https://www.frontify.com/

To illustrate:
> *August is the month when we have fewer page views because more people are on vacation.*
> (one sentence, three clauses, 16 words)

Dividing it into smaller sentences makes it easier for non-natives and machine translations.
> *More people are on vacation in August. Therefore, we have fewer page views.*
> (two sentences, one clause each, 13 words)

If you know a second language, try these two examples in a tool like Google Translate. The odds are that the second one will be more clearly translated.

To make full use of Kohl's guide, you need to be able to identify grammatical constructs such as relative clauses and participial phrases. To adhere to style guidelines like these in-house, you're going to need some tools and possibly some grammar nerds.

English outside the Anglo-American world

I was an English teacher in the Czech Republic in the early 1990s, and back then English departments debated whether they should be teaching US or British English. Students wondered which variation to focus on.

Today that debate seems quaint. English is much bigger than the countries where it's spoken natively, and a different kind of English has evolved. Every day, countless conference calls go on in English without a single native speaker.

I've heard non-native speakers using invented, self-deprecating names to refer to their unique dialect of English. Examples include Denglish (English spoken by Germans), Freunglish (the English of the French), and Spanglish. A Warsaw native in Chicago invented the word Pogwish to describe the English spoken in the large Polish community there.

As funny as I find these names, these dialects have influence, and non-native neologisms can spread regionally or through an organization. A beamer in the US refers to a BMW. Borrowed from Denglish, beamer is the word for projector, and it has spread through Northern Europe. A beamer or a beamer remote is often what Europeans are looking for to start a meeting. It confuses Americans, but getting people in European settings to use the word projector is like trying to descend crowded subway stairs at rush hour.

When non-native speakers create English content, words like beamer unconsciously slip in. At World Cup time, Germans will publicize places for "public viewing" (that's not a translation; they write it in English). They mean outdoor places where games will be projected on screens, but in the US, a public viewing is associated with funerals. One client's intranet shared globally an interactive tournament guide created by its German office. It was well-made and popular across Europe and the US, but it had confusing references to public viewing. English content created by your network should be reviewed and localized before it's shared globally.

CHAPTER 10
Making Visuals More Adaptable

Few companies maintain creative services departments large enough to make all content look good. In Chapter 7, I looked at four models for delivering such services and explained how to combine them in a localization program. No matter which models you deploy, quality visuals require investment, and since budgets are so hard fought, it's important to get the most from the expense.

Alan Oram is co-founder of Alive With Ideas,[1] a digital creative agency in the UK that blogs frequently on employee communications.

He told me that in retail he has seen corporate offices send promotional-looking materials to stores that were meant to be consumed only internally. Those materials ended up in shop windows—seen by all, but ignored by employees. "When walking through an office or working environment, there are occasions when it's hard to know if a communication was created for external audiences or was aimed at employees," he said. "Developing a brand is about consistency, but the brand should be flexible enough to work for all audiences and stakeholders. An internal communication must stand out and hold attention but be clearly targeted to its audience."

Connecting designers with users

Whether done in-house or through a vendor, creating visual elements almost always falls to Corporate or regional offices because that's where the resources are. I spoke with directors at creative agencies about how their work process changes when the client is a global business. They all said that they typically manage visuals centrally, using templates under their control. To adapt content for other languages, they create multiple versions and turn to local business units for review and quality control.

---

[1] http://www.alivewithideas.com/

However, managing visuals centrally doesn't mean that creation has to be top-down. Even when local sites lack skilled designers, you can get close to co-creation by seeking user input during the creation process.

"Anytime you're developing a template or any kind of visual system that can be populated with different kinds of information, people who will be using it should be involved in the development," said Arlene Birt. "It's the basis of design thinking. At the very beginning, designers have to think of the end audience and the context for the result."

Designers must know early on what kind of business their users are in, how they work every day, and what tools they have access to. "If something is to be implemented in five countries, then each of those countries should have input during development," she said. "That tells designers about cultural differences, perception and interpretation, how each country will use the material, and the business scenarios for each of those countries. It's important to understand those scenarios during the creation of visual tools and templates."

Invest in time for user input

Mistakenly seen as too expensive, budgeting time for user dialogue and review ultimately saves money because it prevents re-work and protects your investment.

In the same way that it's ridiculously expensive to rewrite something already at the printer, big changes in design can cost you if they come too late in the process. Said Birt, "First we *sketch* ideas for a concept and *wireframe* content. We typically gut-check these with our clients. Then we develop the design in a digital format. After you've completed the design development phase, it's resource intensive to redo the concept. Some types of smaller edits during later phases are possible—including during the implementation of the design—but once you've built the house, it's expensive to move the walls around."

User input should be more intensive than a one-time focus group. If I were asked how I completed a routine task, important details might occur to me later. Giving people additional time to think through how they use a tool in actual practice will help get you better feedback.

To provide useful feedback, it helps when target groups get familiar with the design process. "The earlier you can involve people the better, because they may require a little training to work through the whole process. We have to guide them to give us feedback based on the stage that we're in," said Birt. "*Storyboards* for example, are a concept, not the end design. When we bring in policy experts to look at a storyboard, they can get hung up on visual details that we haven't yet arrived to in the design."

Meaningful dialogue makes the entire process more collaborative, and the learning goes both ways. Designers learn about business use, and users learn about design processes and sound principles of *user-centered design*.

Co-creating with templates and brand guidelines

Many companies have a detailed manual that outlines their brand guidelines, with instructions on the color palette, use of the logo, standard layouts, and so on. These guidelines are a thoroughly thought-through universe, representing the best work of creative agencies.

And they get ignored every day.

Detailed brand guidelines can be off-putting to those outside the design world. While marketing and brand teams are familiar with the language of visual specifications, brand guidelines can leave other functions a little bewildered.

As a result, most companies provide a library of templates, which is what busy employees prefer, as long as those assets suit their purpose and are easy to find and use. If you don't make it easy, one-off requests for brand support from local business functions can quickly overwhelm creative resources at Corporate.

Or worse, people will create their own. This output is often not only non-compliant with brand standards, it's a waste of employees' time and squanders whatever the company has invested in creative assets.

So what is it to be? Give them fish or teach them to fish for themselves?

Balancing fixed and flexible brand elements

Organizations are full of people who see themselves as creative, and with good intentions, they make bold and sometimes awful decisions.

"The question of how to maintain a brand comes up frequently," said Oram. "What elements can be manipulated, project by project, location by location? Guidelines should define where we—and others—are allowed to play. Creating some sort of differentiation between communications is essential so we need to point out where there is flexibility in the guidelines. Part of our job is to encourage people to unlock that flexibility in an effort to keep communications fresh. Maybe it's to change the tone, be playful with the subject matter or use a different style of illustration. Brands and brand guidelines shouldn't be so prescriptive that they put a stranglehold on internal communication. It's about defining the constants and the variables within the approach."

One approach to encourage variety is to provide a richer assortment of examples. A senior designer told me he was developing a playbook to show a client's employees how to visually work with the brand.

"We decided not to offer templates because people tend to go for certain design tricks they like, and over time everything starts to look the same. We want them to understand that communications can look very different and still be on brand. Our client's local practitioners aren't professional designers, so we're going beyond guidelines and creating an inspirational look book. We show different iterations where the main element is typography, photography, or color. Showing how to play gives local agencies more freedom," he said.

Creating and maintaining a design system language

Once a *brand identity* with standards and templates is in place, companies hope that it will proliferate throughout the organization. While the use of templated presentations often grows, designers skilled enough to create new visual content may reside only at headquarters.

The best way to proliferate a brand identity into various markets is to hire skilled designers wherever content is needed. But since design staff can be expensive, the most affordable and efficient way to provide these skills to the business may be through creative resources based in regional offices.

Designers understand brand methodology, patterns, colors, font families,[2] and visual tone. Skilled professionals can help local countries express the brand, balancing consistency and local impact. The design team can be small, but if they're all located in the corporate office, they'll be less aware of local standards—such as paper size—and they can be easily overwhelmed. Instead, a few creative resources in regional offices and adjacent time zones can better manage the variety of needs.

Designing consistently with dispersed, globally diverse teams requires a *design system language* (DSL). A DSL helps designers manage local complexities and transfer design knowledge to local units. According to Alan Power, "The main goal of a design language is to create focus and clarity for designers. A design language is like any language. If there is any confusion it will cause a breakdown in communication"[42].

Like any language, DSL can be translated into other cultures, and you can adapt different aspects of the brand identity in stages. Power continues, "It's up to you as to how many elements you take at a time, but you should never bite off too much. It will just distract you from really focusing on the smaller details. My starting preference would be—colours, typography // icons, input fields // tables, lists // etc."

---

[2] The homepage of Netherlands-based Typotheque demonstrates how font families work with multiple languages (https://www.typotheque.com/fonts/global).

A DSL will grow and evolve, and with flexible visual components, the depth of localized branded content will also grow. "The creation of the style guide and in turn the development of a component library is the evolution of a design system," he wrote.[3]

Localizing with templates and guidelines

Offices providing creative services for international consumption have options for delivery, ranging from traditional and centralized to more ambitiously decentralized.

Option 1: tight control

Judging by the designers I know, this is the most common practice. They create centrally and manage various layouts themselves. With this workflow, designers are given translations and they flow them into place.

The disadvantage is that no one person can recognize whether the translations in layout are correct. For example, non-native speakers creating English content often don't know that word breaks can't be arbitrary. Similarly, unless you're fluent in the target language, you may not recognize headings and subheadings.

With centralized creation, the onus is on the organization (not the designer) to ensure that the text is accurate. This is a two-step process. First you have to manage the text translation, and then you have to get a proper local review at the right stage in visual production.

Option 2: local templates

Creating templates with fixed visuals but flexible text is an initial step toward getting countries involved in their own localization. These kinds of templates should make it easy for users to modify text. They must be attractive, easy to work with, and usable by staff with different levels of skill.

---

[3] According to Swetha Suresh, "Having a design language in place enables a team of designers, developers and every other interdependent group in the digital ecosystem to create, recreate, modify or iterate on a product in a quick and cost efficient manner"[51].

Templates should have lots of white space to accommodate text expansion in target languages, and they should come with instructions for workarounds in case the content overflows the allotted space.

Create templates that people can use in common applications like those in the Microsoft Office suite, but also consider user workflow. Templates created in Microsoft Word may make content accessible to many users, but that content isn't always portable to other tools, operating systems, and publishing platforms.

Birt recommends user training, even for content in familiar applications. While templates sound easy, she cautions that they can be tricky. She said that getting Word templates to work for all users and all their versions of Word is difficult, and PowerPoint templates can't be printed consistently and are too easy for users to change.

"A good designer has the training necessary to develop visuals in a way that audiences will be able to walk away with the intended message. But user modifications can bring the whole brand style out of whack. Anytime someone who's not trained in design works with documents, whether they're comfortable with the application or not, they can start changing things that a designer knows better not to," she said.

Allocating enough space in templates

Designers have to know which language sets they need so they can find font collections that present content correctly. This also helps them allocate space for each translation. Some languages require higher word counts than English (up to 20 percent), and some can be shorter. If they know ahead of time, designers can take these space needs into consideration.

If you're doing multiple-language versions in-house and can't afford multiple designs, I recommend assuming all translations are going to need more space. I have always found translated versions to be longer because the content must explain expressions that are just one or two words in the source language.

Option 3: detailed brand guidelines
Most companies have detailed guidelines for using visual elements of the brand identity. These guideline documents are quite technical, and local marketing and sales departments often hand them off to vendors who know exactly how to interpret the specifications to ensure that layouts are correct and suitable for local needs.

While managing multiple designs has great creative potential and possibly more local impact, it can be impractical for employee communications to work with multiple firms. Birt said that coordinating layouts with agencies and freelancers in multiple countries is the most time-intensive option, and employee communications typically can't afford that complexity.

In theory, employees in local businesses could follow brand guidelines and create their own unique materials. This is co-creation, and doing it right requires more investment.

Option 4: advanced, flexible tools
Tools such as Beautiful.AI,[4] Prezi,[5] and Canva[6] create a hybrid that allows non-designers to insert branded elements and explore more sophisticated layouts.

"A designer can set up the style and provide a library of brand images that each country can select from. Local markets can provide additional images to make template content country-specific," Birt said. "The difficulty becomes framing what non-designers are allowed to do. We don't want them to hinder the legibility of the text or visuals. These more flexible tools are still being figured out. Some of these tools don't work well together, and they can take a lot of training."

Combining the four options
In practice, companies choose from a mix of these four options depending on each location's ability to execute. In building a blended network of co-creators, localizers, and cascaders, you'll have people close to each local

---
[4] https://www.beautiful.ai/
[5] https://prezi.com/
[6] https://www.canva.com/

business who can assess the relevance of content, adapt if needed, and share appropriately.

> Every stage of developing visuals is an opportunity to work with and train your local network, and regardless of their background, show them how to apply the user-centered principles of *design thinking*.

Even if you provide design services centrally, you can facilitate better local visuals. You can start improving local execution right away simply by involving users in early design stages and training them in how to use the final product.

> Whether you're creating with controlled templates or just offering creative guidelines, designers recommend training users.

Very few business people have design expertise to make visual elements attractive. Unless you train them to use the tools you provide, they can develop bad habits and off-brand output can multiply.

"People will revert to their ways of hand-creating content," said Ann Rockley in an interview. "They'll put bold and italics where they think it should go, put into it what they feel needs to be there. They feel templates are restrictive, so they need to be shown the value of them. If they can't see the benefits, to themselves or to people reading content, they will take the easiest path."

To advance communication skills in the business, your network should be engaging frequently with local colleagues about their information needs and their creative choices.

Part III Conclusion

The steps outlined in Part III are either free, won't cost you a lot of money, or offer savings if you implement them. They are important habits that every global organization must develop. Even if your company can't afford the time and energy for localization, or if a merger or some other major event doesn't allow you to focus on localization in the short term, you still can communicate better. English mastery has made the world smaller, but technologies that deliver consumer experiences according to user preferences are evolving fast. If you allow routine, provincial practices to continue, your reach is going to be limited.

Involving others in our process is at the heart of localization. Part IV looks at advanced steps you can take with markets that are ready for more communications responsibility.

Capabilities and Resources

What You'll Learn: The capabilities you need to maintain and the skills your team should develop for localizing communications.

Why You Should Care: If you don't provide a professionalized career path and positive opportunities for collaboration and development, you'll drive away the people you need for an effective network.

CHAPTER 11
Thinking Internationally

Corporate Communications often cites company culture—routinely and explicitly—thinking it's something that everyone feels.

They should probably give that a rest. We shouldn't confuse the home-office culture with what we imagine to be a global company culture.

When I told a *change management* trainer with a global pharmaceutical company about the subject of this book, she laughed and said that communications from her US-based headquarters strengthen the local culture. She said colleagues in her European office bond over mocking output from the home office, hardly what Corporate Communications hopes for.

Consultant Leonard Rau has seen it too. "It's a classic clash of big and small, and the only way local culture gets some control over a situation is to reject it. They don't have power, they feel threatened, and their view is 'I'm not going to trust this big corporate thing coming at me.' Driving messaging from a paternalistic point of view won't work anymore. You have to recognize that clash and complete some genuine localization and tailoring. You must find ways to align incentives so that there's something in it for both the company and the local business."

When corporate asks people to behave in ways that are incongruent with the local culture, their requests seem remote and unnatural. One American human resources manager told me that when he was based in Spain, people identified more as members of their union than as employees of the company. Their view was that names and logos come and go, but the union is forever. That sentiment may be hard for American management to grasp, but for that industry in Spain, it would be stupid to ignore.

Although the idea of a unified corporate culture persists, local culture still matters.

> You may see headquarters as the helm of the ship, but global corporate culture may not be what you think it is, and you may not be able to force it to become what you envision.

In 1980, Geert Hofsted published *Culture's Consequences: International Differences in Work-Related Values*[69], which examined microcultures in 40 international IBM locations (the second edition, published in 2003, covers more than 50). Since then many have added to the discussion on the tension between corporate and local culture. Values hierarchies are beyond the scope of this book, but the observation that local culture can trump corporate culture should no longer come as a surprise.[1]

The international mindset

In her PhD thesis, "Intercultural competencies needed by global CEOs"[21], Dr. Barbara Gibson identified five important capabilities that CEOs in a multinational environment must develop in order to combat cultural blinders (abbreviated here):

- **Cultural self-awareness:** know your influences, your biases, and how your culture might be perceived
- **Cultural sensory perception:** be able to spot cultural differences
- **Open-mindedness:** be willing to accept other ways of thinking
- **Global perspective:** see business as transnational, not domestic first
- **Adaptability:** be able to change behavior, communication style, or business strategy to fit the circumstances

Although Gibson focused on leadership, in our interview she said that communication departments should develop these same competencies. "Headquarters can have cultural blinders, and those blinders lead to biases. Even the word 'best practice' has bias. In turn, corporate teams get frustrated because they can't get their points across," she said.

---

[1] "Cross-cultural communication for managers"[35], a 1993 paper by Mary Munter, provides interesting examples of communication styles clashing with local cultures.

In our interview, she cited people's relationship with time as an example. Not all see working into the evening as a virtue, and the budgeting of time in project plans can have bias. "US culture tends to be oriented toward getting something out the door and then fixing it later. Germans tend toward wanting to get it right before launch. If you can be aware of these preferences, you'll make fewer mistakes."

In *Think Outside the Country*[63], John Yunker agrees that habits and attitudes are of central importance to communicators working globally. "While you can't literally think globally, you can be a global generalist—someone who knows a little about a great number of countries and cultures and languages. By focusing on amassing a broad stretch of knowledge, you will be better prepared to ask the right questions about any new product or marketing initiative before taking it global."

He continues, "The globalization of any product and business is by nature a team effort. And global generalists are best positioned to lead their organization to global success." The same applies to internal, global initiatives.

Global conference calls

If a company could do one thing to improve global co-operation, it would be to transform conference calls into something more collaborative.

No one looks forward to them, but for non-native speakers, the experience adds stress. Audio isn't a great medium to combine with language barriers, and people who speak and understand English at a high level still struggle to pick up nuance through tiny speakers. The format favors English-confident extroverts, and many remain silent, unsure that they're correctly following the discussion. Worried about sounding stupid, they stay silent.

This silence is often interpreted as lack of interest, but the quality of the sound, the speed of the conversation, and the relevance of the content combine for an intimidating experience. Video can be an improvement, but not all locations have bandwidth for it, which means many still need to lean forward and yell into a speaker.

The traditional, smothering conference call is still common in most organizations. You can fix this with no additional cost if participants shift to a global mindset. Here are some suggestions for making conference calls more effective:

Before the call:

- Every call should have a moderator who shares an agenda beforehand, keeps people to it, and summarizes major points and next steps after the meeting.
- The moderator should remind participants of international participation. Urge them to slow down their speech, simplify terms, avoid idioms, and speak in complete sentences, loudly and clearly.
- Provide an agenda or a written summary of the call topics. Even a few informal sentences can help people understand what's expected.
- For recurring calls, ask participants for input on the format and agenda.
- Participants at the corporate office often gather in the same room. An in-person meeting is a better experience for them, but the group easily forgets about those not physically present. On the remote side, we struggle to make out what is often just local small talk. Remind those in the room to refrain from banter, and if you have multiple microphones, distribute them around the table.
- Check the feasibility of the time for all locations. Meetings during business hours for US-based headquarters take place in Asia late the evening. Instead, schedule meetings at different times so the pain of taking a call outside of business hours is distributed equally.

During the call:

- Remember that only those sitting near the microphone can be heard. Side chatter is common, and microphones aren't smart enough to pick up the main thread. Although side conversations may seem productive to those in the room, they make headquarters seem clique-y, provincial, and disrespectful of others' time. If they go on at length, people in other locations drift off and check email. Steer side conversations back to include everyone.

- Throughout the call, take every opportunity to recap or re-state what was just said, especially if it was a quiet voice removed from the mic. Repetition is your friend.

After the call:

- Distribute a written summary of what was discussed and decided. Be clear on responsibilities and deadlines.
- If people from your network participated, be sure they understand next steps and any responsibilities they have. If they are clear on what was decided, they can address any misunderstandings locally.

"What can native speakers of English do to improve international conference calls"[1], a blog post from Abbey Communications, has more suggestions that should be shared widely in any English-speaking headquarters.

Using agencies to generate content

When it comes to local-market public relations, many companies have agencies on retainer to manage the complexity of local media, language, and culture. In theory, the same model could be applied to employee communications. But I've never seen it. If agencies are used, it's for short-term projects. Outsourcing content production and adaptation makes sense when:

- It's a sudden need, and you're in a hurry.
- You want something highly visual.
- The project has a mandate to get more attention.

Agencies will almost certainly create content that stands out. But they can do more for you than that. When you use agencies, take note of two potential benefits. First, their perspective as outsiders can be valuable. The questions they ask can reveal issues and opportunities you didn't see.

Second, measuring results for outsourced content gives you a chance to compare using an agency to conventional practice. Communications struggles to provide measurements that are meaningful to the business, and outsourced content is a chance to do some cost/benefit analysis—if you gather data.

Don't forget to measure the results for agency support that's locally procured as well. Take note of countries using local vendors to translate, design, create, or execute. You can get some measurement in place and study the results. A positive outcome following a well-localized campaign can help make the case for expanded localization.

Tread lightly though. If the business unit is lucky enough to have leaders who invest in communications, you don't want to give them the idea that corporate is stepping in to take over. Make it clear you only want insight into what's working and whether the results can be compared to other markets.

Things that can go wrong with vendor content

- **Insufficient initial briefing:** Without a company's early input, agencies make their best guess, and then the deliverable is limited in where it can be used. Too often that's our fault, not theirs. Help your organization direct stakeholder input to the agency so that they can start building an effective concept. Make sure they understand who's going to use the end product. Profile the demographic you're targeting and identify any technical limitations you have in reaching them.
- **No written content until the last minute:** Organizations don't always understand how to work with agencies. They often deliver an initial, inadequate briefing and then disappear. The agency lays out placeholder copy, repeatedly reminding the client that they need input, and then time runs out. Even though you are purchasing content, understand that vendors can't write it on their own. There are some truths only your company knows, and you must define what you want to say. To get there, you may need to pester stakeholders to make sure they provide what the agency needs at the right time. Waiting too long adds to costs and timelines.
- **Tone deafness:** Agencies don't know your employees, the business, or recent history. If a message is going to annoy or worry employees, agencies may not be able to warn you.

- **The costs and scope creep:** If people in employee communications haven't worked with agencies before—which is likely—they may not appreciate the costs of what they're asking agencies to do. Misunderstandings quickly increase the size of invoices (e.g., asking for major revisions late in the process). It's important to prevent these miscues, especially with small budgets.

When to keep content creation internal

Your own people know the business and local context. Examples of when it can be more effective to execute content on your own include:

- Routine or periodic announcements where your current levels of readership, awareness, or action taking are acceptable
- A familiar information reference that people already know how to use
- News on sensitive topics that needs to be explained and contextualized (such as re-organizations or ongoing negotiations over labor contracts)

When you develop content in house, you rely on your own people as a communication channel, which is insourcing's biggest advantage. As you prepare local messengers, you have the opportunity to engage them in the topic and strategy, which is always a good discussion to have.

The content is also more likely to speak your organization's language. It can be processed more efficiently, and depending on the subject matter, it might get you better results with less distortion.

> **Practical Tip: Prepare examples of localized messages**
> Not all managers take to communication tasks naturally. When you distribute materials on global results, share examples of how leaders and managers can link their team's performance to company strategy. Locally generated examples can be more valuable than fixed slides with abstract numbers. Examples of global results from a team perspective, drafted by corporate and provided in a briefing, can inspire local leaders to prepare relevant anecdotes of their own for sharing in face-to-face meetings.

Things that can go wrong with creating content internally

- **There's no money and you have to do it yourself:** A limited or non-existent budget is a reality for many in employee communications. It's common for teams to create videos, *town hall* meetings, webinars, and online news almost entirely on their own. Since creating content is largely what they know, it's understandable if their first instinct is to create more. It's also what their internal customers expect (i.e., "We have a problem, and we need you to write an article about it."). The demand for more and more content can become overwhelming.

  And yet that content may not have much impact beyond the home country. If they're regularly asked to deliver global content using just the team at headquarters, look at the international readership numbers. Once you understand how low the global response is to global content, creating high volumes of it will seem less urgent. You'll have a better argument for focusing less on international articles and more on what you can do to help overseas managers in their team meetings.

- **Communicating change:** *Change management* is a specialization in itself, with experts and consultants who have studied psychology and know how to deal with resistance. They focus on getting employee input and winning acceptance for mergers, re-organizations, and changes to processes, systems, and tools.

  Corporate Communications probably has experience working with change managers, so they may be able to predict when to apply change management methods. If corporate communicators have advance notice, they can provide early support with messaging strategy and delivery. Communication agencies can also help with communicating change, especially if they have a practice devoted to it.

Unfortunately, change management consultants aren't often available to local offices. It's easy for local businesses to underestimate the impact of announcing a change, and if they don't have adequate communications resources or support from Corporate Communications and its agencies, such an announcement can contribute to unrest and works council issues.

- **Sudden, surprise initiatives:** You need to be sensitive as to how often you call on your informal network. Don't make a habit of asking your network to turn tasks around in a short time frame. Your network often sees their work on corporate's behalf as moonlighting while continuing their day jobs. Translation, formatting, and delivery take longer than you might think, especially since they may not have the tools or expertise needed to handle a job as quickly as a full-time professional can.
- **Local business goals:** Because of factors such as local regulations and compensation structures, financial incentives are rarely identical globally. Moreover, the local business unit's key performance indicators (KPIs) usually aren't the same as corporate's. As a result, the numbers that business units pursue probably don't align with what employee communications is measuring in its content. Making the most of global communications deliverables isn't a local priority.

Insourced or outsourced, prepare a briefing

Whether insourcing or outsourcing content, a good briefing mitigates the risks of wasted communications effort. Instead of just describing the deliverables you're hoping for, a briefing should provide meaningful context. It should outline the purpose of a campaign, who it's trying to reach—including demographics—and how success will be measured. Like all good communications, those briefings need to be tailored to the audience.

- When you source internally, you need to account for the skills of your messengers and focus on how you can motivate them.

- When you source externally, you need to prepare an even more thorough contextual brief about who you're trying to reach, why it's important, recent history, expectations, and potential barriers.

> **Practical Tip: Prepare a precise brief**
>
> Creative vendors need your insight to do their best work, but a document dump is not a brief. Long presentations prepared for executives or other internal groups have only small parts that are relevant to an agency.
>
> If you expect them to study several long documents, presentations, and videos, it will cost you. You don't want to be billed for time they spend flipping through material that's only tangentially useful. This also dilutes their concentration. Having worked as a freelance copywriter, I know that most billable time for projects is devoted to research. Curate the background that you want them to read. Focus on giving them only the most meaningful information, and make sure what you give them is insightful to people outside your industry. Taking the time to fully explain and frame your pain point will lower the invoice and get you better work.

CHAPTER 12
Photography, Video, and Digital Signage

Conventional wisdom says that devices are getting cheaper, video and editing tools are getting easier to use, and our culture is more and more inclined to share. We all know photographers and Instagrammers. You'd think getting interesting photos and usable videos from the field would be easier than ever.

You'd be wrong.

As advanced as the technology is, good shots of employees are frustratingly hard to come by. Journalistic camera skills are rare, and it takes a special kind of photographer to capture people in real-world, dynamic settings, put the subjects at ease, and get a lens pointed in the direction of their faces. I'm not that kind of photographer, and that's why my photo library is filled with landscapes, buildings, and the backs of people's heads.

And yet there's high demand for authentic photos and video, so internal resources are often assigned to get them. It sounds easy, but the real-world images that they shoot are limited. Security often prohibits photos in industrial settings, so office employees get disproportionately represented.

What you end up with are shots of people touring a facility (taken from behind), a motionless group sitting around a conference table in a dark room, or my favorite, a group cheerlessly standing against an office wall like a police lineup. The people depicted are not identified and, because some were visitors, not all of them can be chased down, either to name them or to get them to sign a *photo release*. To add insult, there's a time-and-date stamp in the lower right corner.

Events are especially problematic. When you know about them in advance, you can ask somebody to be there with a camera. But often the photographer gets roped into supporting event planners. They become too busy with the day's logistics and forget to take photos. The only shots taken are afterthoughts or lineups of tired people posed with trophies or certificates as the event comes to a close. Personally, I find nothing duller than a photo of award winners posing shyly with the Great Leader, and I doubt I'm alone. Unfortunately, after the fact, it's a missed opportunity that can't be fixed.

These challenges complicate things for companies whose brand identity requires photos of people in real-world settings. I'm all for brands shunning stock photography, but getting suitable photos takes effort and skill.

People shots aren't the only challenge. One client in the hospitality industry encouraged employees to share real-life shots of their cocktails and dishes on Instagram. The results made it clear why there's a profession specializing in food photography. No matter how good those experiences were in real life, few of the amateur shots were appealing—and many looked disgusting. It wasn't exactly in keeping with the brand promise.

These issues are multiplied when it comes to video. Research suggests that mimicking television-quality video isn't always successful, and flawed but authentic video has power. However, it is a hassle to edit crowd-sourced video, as Mark Ohlsen described in Chapter 4. Poor lighting and microphone placement make most amateur video hard to watch. I've seen leaders do selfie videos silhouetted against a window in a skyscraper, thinking the dramatic setting would be compelling. But the results were so back lit that it looked like the speakers were in a witness protection program.

Another common problem is capturing spoken word. If you record a speech from the back of the room using a phone, the audio sounds like it's coming from the bottom of a well.

> **A professional can help you build a high-quality local photo library.**

Hiring a professional, even occasionally, can go a long way in building a library of high-quality local photography and video assets. "We need local images to match local context," said Arlene Birt. "Freelancers are a great resource, especially for photography. It can be cheaper than purchasing quality stock images one by one."

Professional photography and video can improve the overall look and feel of local communications, and establishing a relationship with a local photographer can have long-term benefits. As the photographer gets to know the business, and as local businesses get to know what a photographer needs during a shoot, they can work together to deepen their library of images. Photographers working locally are also more attuned to the culture outside of the business, so they'll know more about compelling settings, events, and other opportunities to place the brand and capture unique photos.

Local, professionally sourced photos also save people time. Instead of searching the corporate library for something that isn't there—and ultimately settling for another alien-looking photo—local staff can quickly get something suitable to their culture. When you factor in the impact and the improvement in productivity, local professional photographers aren't that expensive.

Because of the appeal of visuals, leadership might be more easily persuaded to spend a little money to source photography and video. It's also a way to get local participation and ownership. If a country complains that imagery is too corporate or too American, use it as a lever to get local investment. Once the photos are taken, your network contact can make sure that they are accessible and legal to use in the global library (and appropriately identified, tagged, and linked with metadata so they can be found by others).

> **Practical Tip**
>
> For events, assign a skilled photographer/videographer—or hire a pro—and have them wander. The best people photos are in the moment, and getting images should be that person's only focus. Arrange for formal photo shoots in local markets regularly. If you have just one shoot every couple of years, the images will go stale quickly.

Image vacuums and lawsuit risks

Ideally, content creators have access to a good, deep photo library. Traditional image repositories have been difficult to maintain, because the bigger the library, the bigger the headaches in keeping it stocked with useful, timely and legally permitted images.

When the European Union's *General Data Protection Regulation (GDPR)* went into effect in early 2018, organizations started to become more stringent about permission signatures for those depicted.

> Post-GDPR, organizations all over the world are paying closer attention to usage rights.

If your brand identity is photography driven, providing legally usable, on-brand photos is a must. If you can't provide local countries with easy access to photos that they want to use, employees will search online, and unauthorized images will make their ways into presentations and internally created posters. The same is true for music. It's easy for employees to create a video, set it with a popular song not authorized for commercial use, and post it on YouTube. You don't want to find out about such a video the hard way.

People outside the communications profession may find this caution overly paranoid. Individuals may get away with violating commercial-use laws, but if you're a global brand, your company's pockets look deep, and that makes you a target for lawsuits. Don't believe me? Have a look at this blog post from the Content Factory about their unpleasant experience with an author photo and copyright infringement: "The $8,000 Mistake That All Bloggers Should Beware"[15].

Large commercial image banks aggressively pursue monetary damages for unauthorized use. "Cookies and tracking software keep images in their sights, and they can call you the day the rights expire. Content has been monetized and they're going to be much more aggressive," one communications consultant specializing in intellectual property rights told me.

Regulations are also moving to protect image owners. New European laws[1] seem to be facilitating the pursuit of financial damages; if your web site is visible in Europe, it will have to comply.

---

[1] See "Online photos can't simply be re-published, EU court rules"[14] and "Photography Copyright in Europe"[41].

In fact, you need to be aware of plagiarism in all its forms, including written content. Your content in all languages needs to be authentic and original (or properly cited). Online content quality and grammar reviewers like Grammarly and ProWritingAid can also check content to see if any portion of it has been published previously on the web.

Laws on intellectual property are complex and vary by country. If you rely on third parties or local talent to understand copyright law on their own, you may run afoul of the law. Your network must know how to source and use content that is free of legal risk. They also need to be aware of limitations so that they can look out for copyright infringement in work created by colleagues. Self-sufficiency and well-trained eyes need to be part of your localization program.

Effective tools to protect you from violations and lawsuits are available, but like all tools, users must be trained to use them. Tools such as Google Image Search[2] can help users determine whether an image has been used previously online, and newer services like Promo[3] allow you to build assets from a template library, with royalty-free licensed images, video, and music. Services like these are especially attractive for smaller organizations with smaller budgets and less knowledge about image use regulations.

> Practical Tip: Enabling local video
> Easier tools could encourage more video production and sharing, and apps that enable this are becoming more accessible. For example, Clipisode[4] allows users to collect and share video responses to specific questions and weave them into short branded videos. This capability would be especially useful in local-language markets that don't produce their own video due to costs, and who otherwise consume only localized corporate videos (i.e., subtitled). Clipisode is free to download and use and can be a good first step for teams that have little knowledge or experience producing video.

---

[2] https://images.google.com/
[3] https://promo.com
[4] https://clipisode.com/

Operations and images

Good pictures of employees on the job are rare. When you get a good one, it's crushing to find out that you can't use it. You may need to reject otherwise good photos and videos because they have a background your corporate policy finds inappropriate, show dangerous or illegal behavior, or portray acts that employees are trained to avoid. Even if it's a minor infraction, it doesn't help if you feature images that depart from your company's brand, policies, and training. I've seen photos rejected for showing someone using a tool incorrectly, driving with one hand or while on the phone, or leaving a shop floor unclean.[5]

Communicators in remote locations, away from operations and its routine training, don't always spot content that violates these rules. As you learn of images that are unacceptable to operations, share the criteria with your network because they may not recognize the violations either. More likely though, the network will be able to train you at corporate—they've probably had more local safety training than people at headquarters, and that's a learning opportunity for the entire communications team.

You should continually discuss what is acceptable and unacceptable with your network. If each person in your network works in isolation, you each learn independently, duplicating effort. If you learn as a team, everyone learns faster.

The limits of a photo library

Given the challenges of image quality and legality of use, it's tempting to try and control which photos can be used. Making photo assets available to your network is generally a good idea, but mandating which ones to use is a bad one.

Your network's main task should be to create content that's appropriate for their audience, and as Val Swisher points out, appropriate content includes the selection of images, symbols, icons, and photos.

---

[5] "Beware the Photo Shoot"[31] describes a case where a toy gun wasn't noticed in the background until it was too late.

In addition to the pitfalls described above and in Chapter 4, some images that we don't give a second thought to can be offensive to some cultures. Swisher advises that you not use any image with hand gestures for global distribution (e.g., one culture's "good job" is another's obscenity), and that you remember that the amount of clothing on models can also be a problem. Bikinis in images for the Middle East would be an obvious example, but Alan J. Porter told me how a photo of a construction worker with his sleeves rolled up caused a problem in Australia, where the safety code requires that sleeves be worn at all times. The photo seemed to be promoting a safety violation.

No one person can possibly know all of the world's cultural norms. It's better to have a wide range of usable visual assets that local content creators can easily access.

Porter told me that many companies struggle to manage visual assets on multiple *DAMs*. Or they mistakenly believe that the asset database within their CMS is a DAM. Unless those assets can be simultaneously accessible to other publishing tools, it's not. The need for simplicity, and the costs and risk of the status quo, may bring about more comprehensive solutions. Citing Nuxio[6] as an example, he said, "The rise of content services platforms is where things are likely to go. That would be something like a DAM that also has the ability to do federated search across the metadata of other repositories."

New solutions may help, but current tools may already have many of the capabilities you need to locate images easily. Regardless, you need people trained in maintaining images.

"You have to engineer the content in the first place to be findable," said Porter. "Instead of files named by the system as 1234.jpeg, you've got to put together a tagging scheme and a taxonomy and determine who applies metadata—whether you leave it to users, who hate putting in metadata and filling in forms, or put it in automatically, pulling metadata in from other

---

[6] https://www.nuxeo.com/

systems. Companies are starting to realize that they can make content findable with the right metadata and a good taxonomy."

Images and video are central to the media that Communications works with, and making your assets findable and usable might be a worthwhile joint effort across your company. If communicators throughout your company were responsible for using a good taxonomy and applying metadata to the assets in your DAM or repository, you would reduce the risks of unauthorized image use, make more effective visuals available, and contribute to a shared sense of purpose across communications.

All digital signage is local

Digital signage can be powerful and immediate in commanding attention, and it can be a good way to reach non-wired, on-location employees in industrial and retail settings. It can range in sophistication from networked screens managed centrally to a single screen fed with a USB stick.

Hardware prices have come down enough that digital signs are no longer a huge investment. But when local managers talk about installing a large screen to get their messages across to employees, I break into a sweat. They're so in love with the idea that they often jump in too soon, underestimating how much time and resources it takes to create an effective channel.

As with many well-meaning new vehicles, people in Communications get to be the killjoy. We warn them that after being installed with great enthusiasm, signage often devolves into stale content that sits there for weeks on end, slipping into a background that's easily ignored. Managers need to understand why they shouldn't rush into digital signage without assessing how they'll use it and assigning ownership.

Poor execution can make electronic signs truly awful, and the worst-case scenarios go beyond having little to no impact. Outdated content sends an unintentionally demotivating message: we don't care about you enough to update this. Stale content can contribute to communication problems and employee dissatisfaction.

Sean Matthews is the president and CEO of Visix,[7] a US-based company providing digital signage solutions in corporate, educational, healthcare, and government settings. "People inevitably underestimate how much time and money it takes to feed fresh, compelling content to screens on a daily basis," he said. "Hanging a display on the wall and just running a PowerPoint presentation is a mistake."

Start planning for it now

Maintaining signage is like creating a weekly video newsletter, but despite being warned of this, local managers often pull the trigger anyway. Whether you want it or not, screens are going to continue popping up at local sites, so I recommend getting a plan ready for creating and sharing screen content now. Without a plan, it's going to be hard to influence content quality beyond the screens you directly control, especially if they're in far-off facilities.

To create good video content, corporate can obviously be a partner. But it can also be a barrier. Matthews said, "The bureaucracy is not typically focused on what a local office needs or wants to say, but is centered on IT policy. The sad reality is that most large-scale deployments are driven by IT personnel and policies. The stated mission of delivering relevant, timely and influential content to target audiences gets lost to an IT department that is concerned about uptime, trouble tickets, and security policies."

Bureaucratic delays and lengthy approvals encourage rogue installations, especially since low-priced local solutions are readily available. Corporate needs to engage local management ahead of time and help them understand that managing digital signs doesn't happen automatically. Nor should corporate insist on entirely centralized content, because if nothing else, the occasional use of the space for *babies and birthdays* gets more attention. "At a technical or IT level, it makes sense to centralize control because you want to ensure network integrity," said Matthews. "But any digital signage solution should enable local content contribution and ownership. It's a common feature because it's essential to successful signage."

---

[7] https://www.visix.com/

Matthews says there's a strong tendency for corporate to hijack local channels like these. Governance and sharing content responsibilities can aggravate tension between local sites and corporate, and co-operation will take negotiation.

Remember that local management had good reasons for wanting screens in their facilities. While their enthusiasm may be mostly related to costs they see as low, they may also feel that traditional, global channels aren't having an impact. If their needs aren't well served by global content in English, if they have a higher proportion of employees who don't work at computers, or if their teams say that they don't see news despite it being published in every global channel, they may want to give local screens a try. Approach these discussions with the value you can provide rather than the control you want to exert.

Developing quality signage content on an ongoing basis

Content is the core challenge to any system of communications, and there has to be a sustained commitment to developing it. In local business units, the skills to create video content and deploy it effectively are often even harder to come by than traditional communication skills. And yet, it's also common to find enthusiastic amateurs from outside communications who love video and want to practice. Tapping into their enthusiasm and assuring message integrity is a balance.

The initial skills gap in digital signage is an opportunity for corporate and the local network to provide better support. While I believe the risks of a half-effort are high, stepping up and providing support is an opportunity for corporate to shore up local communications and possibly jumpstart your first channels with localized content.

> Managing an effective digital signage channel is a microcosm for localizing employee communications.

Using digital signs effectively requires clear determination on whether control is central or local. It needs a clear process for high-quality, attention-getting content. As with the other processes that I've been advocating throughout this book, you need dedicated staff and a scheme for them to be continuously learning and improving. You'll need a calendar, a bank of images, and templates and assets that can be localized.

Whether it's implementing a new system or leveraging scattered screens that you already have, feeding video-ready content can serve as a pilot for localization practices. It provides a chance to work together, define and share best practice, establish tools for co-creation, and measure results.

Think guidance and setup rather than daily content
With an up-front investment of time, you can help local owners sustain content creation that needs little intervention from you or even them. Content areas you should help set up include the following:

- **A feed with updated local performance measures:** Rather than just the occasional local human resources notification and lunch menus, signage can also share local business results. Visix advises its clients to share key performance indicators (KPIs) onscreen. Publishing performance measures helps with motivation and connects more directly to local strategy. People's genuine interest in the numbers keeps the channel alive.

- **Support for interactivity and a consumer-like experience:** Matthews said that people increasingly expect interactivity, and technology increasingly supports it. In any setting, including the workplace, individual viewers want to select the content they're interested in. You can set up newsfeeds, directories, and maps that require minimal maintenance. "This is localization down to the person," Matthews said, "Users want this more and more, and the system set up just isn't that difficult."[8]

Some people are more suited to maintaining signage than others. Building a good channel may be more viable where you have people with enthusiasm and willingness to play with functionality. Matthews says that some of their clients are lucky to find local signage owners who embrace the potential and work on deepening their skills to make it continually better.

---

[8] In "Using Interactive Digital Signage to Increase Customer Engagement" [16], *Digital Signage Today* offers a summary of the benefits and challenges of digital signage. They say that without interactivity, people increasingly tune displays out.

University campuses, for example, often have easier access to willing talent. "Campuses are probably the furthest along in adopting a localized approach because they're used to communicating across disparate audiences and channels. Their student viewers demand a continuous stream of changing content like social media feeds, event schedules, and community calendars. In addition to delivering localized communications that people want to see, automated content sources allow communicators to deliver nonstop messaging that's timely and relevant without having to hire additional staff," he said.

> ### Practical Tip
> Optimizing digital signage can be your first foray into localization and co-creation. If you have screens in multiple sites across your organization, try a pilot for co-creating content. If screens have already been in use, local business units will probably jump at the chance for help in feeding the channel.
>
> For more on digital signage best practice, Visix offers four free master class guides[59] on its website, as well as a regular podcast.[9]

---

[9] https://www.visix.com/resources/podcasts/

CHAPTER 13
Leveraging Content from Other Groups

The silos that organizations continually talk about breaking down produce a lot of content, both globally and locally. What employees see as corporate comes not just from Communications, but from a variety of functions, such as operations, IT, compliance, learning and development, human resources, procurement, and more.

Re-purposing content is a good idea, but people underestimate the road blocks. I hear managers shorthand the process as copy-paste. If only it were that easy.

Ann Rockley is a founder of The Rockley Group, a Toronto-based consultancy that helps global organizations develop and implement intelligent content strategies and structured content management. The Rockley Group is known for the Unified Content Strategy^{TM}, a design methodology for structured content and reuse.

Rockley characterizes the time-consuming way that most communicators construct content as handcrafting. It's a good description. We assemble bits and pieces of relevant information, draft something for a specific need, seek approvals from multiple stakeholders, keep up with changes and iterations, and ultimately, if we're lucky, publish.

Rockley argues that instead of handcrafting, content creation should follow a manufacturing model, producing small, granular modules of content designed for re-purposing. The Rockley Group first developed the model for technology companies that frequently update technical documentation and user support content in multiple languages, for various audiences on various channels.

She told me in an interview that whether you implement formal content management or just check in with other departments periodically, the biggest barriers to re-purposing are organizational. "One of the challenges

I find in re-purposing is the different technology barriers within a company. One group has it in one format and you need it in another. It isn't as easy as 'I'd like to reuse that.'" Even linking to existing content has roadblocks, with valuable content available only to group members on platforms such as SharePoint.

> The way content is created today (with multiple versions for different mobile platforms, different versions for different web browsers, tweaks for PDF web distribution, as well as slightly different versions for each eReader environment) is untenable. It's as if we're in the pre-industrial age, handcrafting expensive artisanal products. With the proliferation of mobile devices, that task isn't getting any easier.
> —*Managing Enterprise Content: A Unified Content Strategy, Second Edition*[44]

Implementing new *content models* won't be easy, but there's a strong economic argument in getting more from the effort we're already putting in. Ready-made, localized messaging has many uses, and so cost savings, but executives deciding on funding may be more persuaded by the promise of localized sales content. "People in sales love it if they can quickly pull together a proposal, speech, a slide deck, or something else because they have the ability to re-purpose content. They can put proposals together much quicker and more effectively," she said in an interview.

> **Practical Tip: Tune into what users are doing with brand**
> Your network can be on the lookout for creative uses that Corporate Communications can replicate or improve. A central brand team can tweak local creations and make them available in usable formats for wider distribution. This controlled crowdsourcing deepens the library, reduces the risk of rogue creations, and helps unify a sense of purpose in your team.

Measuring localized content

Measuring global consumption of internal content has unique challenges. Digital channels can provide detailed data, but when it comes to analyzing local use, Corporate Communications doesn't have the time or local insight to comb through and interpret all of it. That's a good reason to keep the network involved in measuring content.

It's not helpful if analytics are available only through a central group in the corporate office. Data reports in pdf format can't be analyzed with flexibility, and getting results is unnecessarily time consuming. Each country should have direct access to measurement tools and be able to track its audience's preferences. They should be able to see for themselves at any time how their local-language content affects their audience's behavior.

> Give each country direct access to measurement tools.

All authors of digital content should be interested in how people engage with their content. This includes learning whether their content attracts new users, how long people spend with their content, whether users view videos, whether subtitling videos helps, and whether users interact with it.

Your network should know how to track if their audience prefers certain themes, subjects, or media types. With one client our team noticed that stories on community involvement got fewer views compared to other types of content. Although several functions in the corporate office expressed interest in the topic, stories in that category were mostly locally created, with low-quality images of volunteers lined up in a group and only spotty information about the charity.

At the same time, we noticed that people were more likely to view recognition in just about any form, especially if employees were named and pictured. So we built recognition into community engagement content and encouraged locally created content to identify and name participants. We saw only a slight uptick in page views, but we saw many more likes and comments.

As a next step, we urged local communicators to incorporate storytelling about the charities to help readers understand the organization, to express what volunteers got from the experience, and to explain what people could do once the event was over. The result was, at least in the short term, increased views. If they continue to do this, they should also track whether participation rates at future volunteer events increase, which is the desired outcome of such content.

Spikes or troughs in content consumption are limited in what they can tell you, but your network can track more meaningful measurements of the overall impact of their content efforts.

Measuring in partnership with your network

Corporate Communications tends to focus on content engagement, but it shouldn't be the network's sole focus when it comes to measurement. Corporate's fixation is somewhat understandable, since it's so hard for global content to prove a link between consumption and business outcomes.

Even when communicators know the results are dubious, they continue to track increases in reads, likes, and comments to prove greater engagement with their campaigns. As Stacey Barr writes in her blog on performance management, corporate's measurement of content has a certain element of CYA (cover your ass):

> "Show you're doing lots of work, doing good things, getting heaps of stuff done.... All you have to do is to find a few measures that always have positive trends and show how well things are going. Measurement drives behaviour, so where do you think people will prioritise their time and attention when they measure the things that are easy to improve?"
> —Stacey Barr, "Why do YOU Measure Performance"[4]

In our interview, Jonathan Phillips said that many communications teams believe their work ends with hitting the send button. "It's an unpleasant truth that some teams are more interested in how many emails they've sent rather than impact. We should be measuring outcomes and not outputs. If you get into the outcomes world, then you can work together. We need a good mutual understanding of metrics and buying into what we are trying to achieve."

At the level of the business unit, local communicators have opportunities that corporate communicators can only dream of: tying their efforts to business outcomes.

To shift local focus away from output and toward outcomes, the network needs to understand the importance of measuring and habitually tracking business results. They should connect with local management and find pain points to which they can apply communications practices. These could include:

- Workplace accidents
- On-boarding vendors
- Reporting results consistently in global trackers
- Sales strategy

Mike Klein has written about tracking "tangible changes in behavior." In *The Present and Future of Internal Comms: How to measure what really matters*[26], he wrote, "One example cited by a practitioner involved a campaign to increase the use of alcohol wipes in a hospital setting—the measurement of which was tracked … through the direct measurement of alcohol wipe usage."

Whatever behavioral problems local leaders are facing, communications can be applied to solving them. Local communicators should focus their energy on changing those behaviors and measuring impact. All results—quantitative and qualitative—should be compared with what was happening prior to the localization program.

The concept of measuring communications may be new to your network. You should ask them what they feel should be monitored, and evaluating results should be a regular part of meetings and one-on-one coaching. Teaching the in-country network to measure communications, and ensuring they follow through on an ongoing basis, accomplishes two things. First, it develops their skills as communications practitioners. Second, it's a great way to build evidence in favor of more investment in your localization and co-creation programs.

> Before you start localization, establish a baseline to get a clear picture of the current state. This will help you evaluate improvement.

> ### Understand is a big word
>
> I was once a novice English teacher, working in Europe with no formal training. My assessment of whether students understood me was intuitive, by what some call the light in their eyes. However subjective this method was, I categorized students into four groups:
>
> - Those who understood
> - Those who thought they understood but heard something entirely different
> - Those who wanted to understand but couldn't
> - Those who didn't care to understand
>
> My instinct was probably mostly right, but educational methodologies rightly demand evidence of student learning. In other words, how do you know that they know?
>
> The same spectrum of comprehension that I patched together as a teacher applies to those taking in corporate content. But from remote cubicles at headquarters, you can't even see their eyes. Thinking ahead about how you're going to know that they know is a good investment.

Finding and supporting brand champions

Almost all companies I've ever worked with have a *brand champions* program. Brand champions are people in the field who advocate for correct use of the brand identity and evangelize on how to maintain its integrity.

Brand champions are put in place due to corporate's distance from business units. "They voice the brand. It's much harder if you push it out from central," said one the brand strategists I interviewed in Chicago. "With local brand champions who feel part of a larger group, it's quicker and easier to implement and change."

Brand champion specifics vary, but I've never seen a scheme that worked particularly well. Brand strategist Leonard Rau told me brand champion programs often go lifeless soon after launch. "The challenge is that the marketing department identifies people they think will be great champions.

The champion asks, 'What do you want me to do?' and the answer is just 'Be a champion. Do what you've always done.'"

He said that the people driving brand ambassador programs forget that in the field, you must earn trust and respect instead of claiming authority and pushing visual compliance. "Unless you equip them with skills and tools to go around championing in ways that are real, it falls flat really quickly."

Having marketing/communications resources perform visual inspections is not what Rau has in mind for brand champion programs. Instead, he said that brand champions should be placed throughout the business.

"Done poorly, brand champion programs are miserable," he said. "Done right they help others really get it. When it works well it empowers people to take an idea and within guidelines, design the new experience. How can you, accountant, change your world based on this new direction? How should you, team leader, conduct your team meetings so that they support the brand? Champions should be asked to create."

Your network should not be brand ambassadors

How your network interacts with and supports brand champions is a good question. On the one hand, collaborating with brand ambassadors can strengthen your network's communications skills and knowledge of brand identity standards.

The tendency though is that local businesses will see the brand program as a policing task, and therefore the responsibility of Communications. Left on their own, local businesses may volunteer your network contact for this thankless role. That person will start getting last-minute brand reviews with pressure from higher-ups to complete them quickly with minimal changes. If the visuals are all wrong, your network contact may not feel empowered to fight the battle.

These are the kind of politics it's best to keep our network protected from. According to Rau, "Policing is less common today, but if you have it, it should be a panel of four to five leaders, experienced people who review work from recent months, deciding what's good and what's not so good.

Those scores can be shared around as models for all the people producing work. The task should be shared more."

Rosie Halfhead said that even in companies where marketing, public relations, and regional communications all have good understanding of the brand, it's a good idea to involve other functions in getting consensus on what that brand should be.

"When doing a brand refresh, we put a brand council together at the outset," she said. "It had multiple representatives at senior levels from across the business regions as well as corporate functions, including IT and operations. As they were all part of the process from the start—including the selection of a supporting agency—they were much more engaged throughout the project and had a vested interest in bringing the refreshed brand to life."

In short, encourage your network to support—but not to become—brand champions. Your people can provide new energy and inspiration, and if the champions are from various disciplines, the program can be used as an almost no-cost professional development opportunity for all involved.

"Communications and brand champions should be part of an integrated team with a clear goal in mind," said Rau. "It should have brand direction from the champions, communication people with authority from corporate and connection to leadership, and sales folks bringing in the voice of customer and product expertise. You've got to see it work across many facets. Otherwise the program ends up being all sales activation and corporate marketing."

Socializing marketing content

Leaders often assume that employees are fully aware of messages aimed at customers. In reality, content is often deployed externally with only a few outside the marketing department seeing it beforehand, if ever.

Not sharing marketing content with employees is a missed opportunity, especially for companies that rely on English as a corporate language. Marketing content is translated and localized much more often, and it may be the only corporate content employees will ever see in their own language.

At the same time, marketing content isn't always compelling to employees on its own, even in the local language. Some employees and cultures view marketing content skeptically. Communications should therefore build a complementary, local context for that content.

Localized content created for external audiences doesn't necessarily need to be re-formatted and re-purposed. Marketing collateral can be a discussion topic for internal teams. Who is the localized marketing piece aimed at, what is the purpose of the product or solution, what is it competing against, what problem does it solves for customers? Team discussions on collateral are valuable opportunities for managers to connect how the team contributes to a larger strategy.

Communications can work together with marketing and sales to provide model talking points for managers to use in team meetings. Rather than top-down scripts, these talking points should serve as examples, and managers should be encouraged to make them their own.

> The discussion about marketing content is localization taken to the team level, and it has more power than any article written by corporate.

Showing management ways to discuss marketing materials is perhaps the best step you can take toward internal localization. Alan Oram advises you to allow enough time. "The power of strong, local connections really comes into play. It's important to provide briefings, templates, toolkits, and useful talking points in advance, so they have time to localize and personalize the messages. Encourage them to take ownership and share their own stories to help bring those comms to life."

Oram agrees that a backgrounder is essential. "It doesn't need to be complicated. A simple guide can help inform them what the campaign is about, what they can expect to see, how they're going to be supported, what's expected of them and helpful tips on how they can support the people they manage."

Oram says the briefing should sketch out scenarios at different levels of the business. "The region manager gets this; the unit manager gets that. Tailor content to their needs so that it's talking directly to them. There will probably be common content for all audiences, but tweak aspects to let them know it's been created for them and try and make it as clear as possible what's expected. If they need to engage in two-way conversations with their teams, then spell it out and give them the confidence and knowledge to do this with some guidance or questions they can ask their teams."

The face-to-face communication channel is often neglected. Some managers will recite briefing content to their teams with a dismissive, passive/aggressive intro: "Corporate wants me to read this to you." But many more will consider your advice and discuss it in ways that suit their personality. The advantages extend beyond message accuracy.

- It makes managers responsible for discussing company strategy.
- The messenger is a local person instead of corporate.
- It connects local results to a global company.
- Communication becomes an act, not a function.
- It demonstrates the value that Communications support can provide.

CHAPTER 14
Tapping into Social Media

After marketing collateral, some of the first channels companies localize are in social media. Like marketing content, social media efforts generally focus on customers and brand reputation. While marketing content is typically created centrally and then translated, social media content is often created locally in the local language. For good and for ill, these teams have more independence from corporate.

Although social media teams don't automatically think to connect with employee communications, most organizations recognize the potential in better coordination across communications disciplines. Nevertheless, it's still frustratingly difficult.

In addition, many companies see brand dilution or brand confusion thanks to competing social channels set up by various locations. Greater coordination between employee communications and social teams can help mitigate this. You may not be able to prevent branded employee posts on Facebook— your company may even encourage them—but your network can promote better practices.

"Global social media is a big issue," said Val Swisher in our interview. "Companies have different communities for different locations in different languages, but there's no cross-pollination. Cheap and instant translation might be acceptable for user-generated social content, but most are still not anywhere near what it needs to be for all the languages they're working in. Companies would benefit from different user constituents all over the world communicating with each other."

If teams can co-operate more, and if internal communications gets involved, you can expand the volume and quality of shared content. For internal communication teams turning to employee-generated content in channels like *Yammer* and *Workplace by Facebook*, that goal is especially worthwhile.

Working with social media teams

Get to know your company's social media teams and the processes they use. Whether they're functioning at a high level or struggling, these teams already know more about what's working and what's not when it comes to localized messaging. You should build an alliance with those publishing in social media, even if it's informal.

In Chapter 6, I proposed that it in small markets it makes sense to have an integrated communications role, where one person or a small team coordinates internal and external communications.

In countries where such people are already in place, find out what they're doing with social media, including which channels they support, what they publish, and how often they publish. In larger markets that devote separate resources to social media, start to develop a relationship. If they work through vendors, work through the vendor's sponsor.

To find potential for collaboration, here are some things you should ask:

- **Which countries have in-language social media teams:** You probably know most of your company's presence in global social channels, but you may be surprised by how many social media communities are maintained locally in various languages. If that content is compelling to customers, it may also be for employees, especially in markets that rarely see corporate content in the local language. If you know where such social media content exists, you can guide employees to it as it's created.

- **How they define and manage their communities:** For each branded social media community that your company runs, someone is managing it. Whether it's in-house or through an agency, they have autonomy to post and respond to comments, and they're trained in the company's tone and social media goals.

  The social media communities they're contributing to will be distinct from employee groups, but their awareness of what kinds of content members contribute or react to can be useful to help you anticipate what kind of reactions your localized employee content might trigger.

- **What sources they draw content from:** Your company's social community managers may be ahead of you in diversifying their sources for content. Learning how they gather these various inputs and what steps they take to adapt it may reveal good sources of corporate content that you weren't aware of. If their network is cross-departmental, it's a potential inroad to people from the business who are willing to evangelize and share content. They could one day become voluntary co-creators of employee content.
- **What can you do for them:** This is where you start the conversation, and what you say could surprise them. Social media practitioners are so focused on their work that they can be unaware of what other countries are doing, let alone internal communications.

But if you can help them develop or curate content, they'll be happy to hear from you. With a sometimes daily need to post, social teams continually look for content they can use or ideas they can develop.

Even if employee communications is less mature in localization and media capabilities, your network will learn of initiatives that might serve as examples. In companies hungry for content, even just a good story lead is a valuable contribution.

Everyone in communications is looking for authentic stories, and employee communications can be a big help with arranging interviews, taking photos remotely, or shooting on-the-job videos.

You can also help social media with their local, internal crowd sourcing. Some companies organize local takeovers of their Instagram channels, where local business units take temporary responsibility for posting content. Without good coaching, the quality of takeovers is hard to control. Global social media teams often provide guidance, but the network may be close by. That means they can offer additional, hands-on expertise with photos and hashtags so that the posts get more traction. For more on running social media takeovers, see "How to Orchestrate a Social Media Takeover from Scratch"[47] by Will Schmidt.

- **Do they want employee participation:** You can help social media teams expand their audience by inviting employees to join. People don't automatically follow their employers in social media, but if they learn that there's content available in their local language, they may become curious. However, before you point employees to a social media channel, get permission from the team that owns it. They may not want employees complaining about work or cheerleading—it may dilute what they're trying to achieve, or they may have metrics that would be disrupted by the extra traffic.

One regional communications head pointed out to me that demographics are changing people's relationships with social corporate content. "A whole new generation has come into organizations who've grown up with different technologies. They're intensely self-creating, intensely interactive. Everyone is creating content themselves, and that's their expectation," she said.

To encourage more collaboration, ask social media teams about their content strategy and ask them to share it with your network. Ask for access to their *editorial calendar* and discuss their upcoming content in your team meetings. Make sure to share with them the photos, videos, and stories that your teams create.

If all goes well, you can share or re-purpose content from social teams to supplement your internal content mix. Closer co-operation between your team and social media will also help you understand employee audiences. As Alan Oram told me, "It's important to consider the bigger picture, remembering the value of listening to conversations that are taking place between employees on social channels—internally and externally—and responding and interacting with them to help shape the conversation."

> **Practical Tip: Localize social media content to team level**
>
> Localization isn't just about a country or a culture. Localization can happen at the team level, where its leaders discuss the broader context behind tasks and results. Social media that's already been localized is an excellent point of team discussion—if they're aware of it. Driving this awareness among local management can be part of your network's responsibility.

CHAPTER 15
Building a Better Team

How people produce content has been the focus of this book, but building an internal communications network has more far-ranging impact than just feeding the intranet. If you build a relationship of trust and collaboration, your network will function as local eyes and ears.

Culture is in the break room

Élise LeMoing Maas is head of the public relations department at the Institut des Hautes Études des Communications Sociales (IHECS) in Brussels. When I asked her about cultural blindness, she said that the voice and tone of global content often reflect the headquarter's culture. As examples, she cited companies depicting time on the job as fun, or offering rewards that take place after hours.

"Work can be pleasant, but it's not the most important objective. For some, dinner with management isn't a gift, it's a work obligation and time away from family. Internal communication is about connectedness. People like their jobs well enough, but they want technical satisfaction and recognition, not a party."

These kinds of missteps are unfortunately common. When I talked with Val Swisher about mistakes corporations make with their translations processes, she said the most common pain point wasn't costs or translation quality, but the company's drive for an emotional connection. She was talking about a brand's relationship to customers, but the same issue applies to companies and their employees.

"Over time, US companies have decided that having customers is no longer good enough. Now companies want customers to be their best friends. This fundamental shift has impacted the way we try to communicate. We are creating content to build a relationship with a long-term emotional commitment. That's not translatable into every language and culture, because not every language and culture wants a new friend. The content can't be translated because it makes no sense to them. Companies are finally waking up to fact that a culture that doesn't want that type of relationship will laugh at content that tries to invoke it," she said. She added that these miscues are best prevented through a distinct process for in-country review.

When clients describe their company culture, they often recite from their brand book instead of personal experience. Aspiration is fine, but your conception of culture should be based on reality.

Maas told me that instead of a declaration, company culture is what people do every day. "Many never leave the workplace, so they don't know the rest of the company. People in communications should try to understand employees' true values and look at how they work in practice," she said.

She said you need to understand local expectations. "Do teams there react to change easily or do they expect to drive change themselves? Are they used to being part of small teams or larger? Is the name of the company important or not? There are many variations on working experience."

These aspects of workplace micro-cultures have a strong influence. Some locations may be mature and well connected to corporate, while others are former partners recently acquired, with fewer resources and less understanding of current wording for what corporate calls its global value proposition. It's tempting to try and tailor deliverables for distinct markets, but in big companies, it's impossible for any global communicator to learn all variations and take them into account simultaneously.

> "Globalization isn't as much about being global as it is about thinking globally. Between wanting to go global and actually going global lies a great stretch of failed websites, wasted money, and lost jobs. Everyone wants to sell their products and services in as many places as possible. But it's the actual process of getting into each country that proves to be the bridge too far for many companies."
> —John Yunker, *Think Outside the Country: a Guide to Going Global and Succeeding in the Translation Economy*[63]

On questions of culture, your network is in a much better position to gauge local sentiment and experience. Rather than just translating corporate words, localization demonstrates to employees that they're valued and makes it easier to communicate the company's aspirations. As Maas put it, "adaptation is a form of respect."

Better network, better outcomes

A network of communicators in local business units can be important allies in just about everything you do, from research to execution to measurement.

"Headquarters is good at broadcasting but less good at listening," said one communications manager working at the European-region level. "How you communicate is particularly important around change and conflict. Even with the most amazing technology, the best way to communicate change and earn support is through smaller, face-to-face sessions where people can interact."

The time, energy, and money you invest in local communication capabilities will improve the entire function for the better. As Ed Catmull says in *Creativity, Inc.*[10], "If you give a good idea to a mediocre team, they will screw it up. If you give a mediocre idea to a brilliant team, they will either fix it or throw it away and come up with something better."

In researching this book and interviewing experts, the notion of a relatively small number of skilled, trained specialists kept coming up, whether it was intranet practices, video localization, or visual design.

Team composition is important, and so is their direct interaction with business units. Yet who local resources are, where they are, and what they can do is only half of the equation. The profession of internal communications continually tries to get a seat at the decision-making table. The second half of the equation is this: can Corporate Communications give network members a seat at their table?

Giving prescriptive instructions to local communicators for every project is micromanaging and unconsciously loaded with cultural assumptions. Relationships between corporate and the network need to be based on empowerment and trust, and the network must benefit from long-term investment. They must continually be brought into the discussion at headquarters and briefed on campaign objectives, strategies, and key messages. If your network participates in these activities, they will work much more effectively when it's time to deliver.

Give your network what they need

A local network needs your ongoing input. Here are some of the most important things you can provide to them:

- **A calendar of what's coming:** Any content team can attest to how important a planning calendar is. It sounds easy, but at time-pressed headquarters, getting ahead of all the agendas is herculean. At corporate we get blindsided by rollouts we weren't aware of and new ideas from on high. Sadly, communications departments are equally guilty of blindsiding their network with sudden campaigns that weren't discussed at the start of the year. A calendar of communication events and initiatives is a must—however imperfect and theoretical. To localize and co-create, people need some idea about what's ahead. No matter how penciled in, you should always work together to sketch out the coming months.[1]

- **A content strategy:** In many settings, a working content strategy feels like a pipe dream.[2] But the more global you are, the more urgently you need one. In *Global Content Strategy*[54], Val Swisher lists a variety of scenarios where a global strategy becomes essential. The first is a four-language test: if you translate content into four or more languages, you need a global content strategy. She also wrote that you need a global content strategy if local offices create content on their own.

---

[1] See Shannon Tien's Hootsuite article, "How to Create a Social Media Content Calendar: Tips and Templates"[57], for guidance on creating a social media editorial calendar.

[2] Rahel Anne Bailie writes in an upland Kapost blog post that content depth and complexity requires moving beyond content strategy to content operations. "…a content strategy is worthless if an organization says 'thank you very much' and pops the carefully crafted, elegant strategy into a drawer to gather dust. If there is no implementation phase, then the strategy is just that: an unimplemented plan." "Leveraging the Natural Connection Between ContentOps and Content Strategy"[3].

Your first pass at outlining a strategy doesn't have to be complicated. If you chart out a calendar for what corporate plans to produce and translate in the short term and add what the local network has in the works, you have a good start. You're well on your way to formulating a content strategy if you involve the network in structuring and honing the outline over time.

- **Key messages for universal topics:** Senior communicators easily connect the dots between news of the day and strategic priorities. It may be some time before everyone in the network knows how to weave general messaging into storytelling. But to help them, they need to be provided with general messaging in the first place.

Our colleagues in public relations routinely prepare key messaging briefs for leadership who will speak at press events. Instead of hiding these briefs in a corporate vault, the core content of those briefings can be re-purposed and made available to the network.

A synopsis of high-level, approved, on-target messaging, organized into categories for various products, services, positioning, and thought leadership gives your network an easy-to-use content playbook. I once shared one of those PR briefs with my network, and it was by far the most popular briefing I ever gave them.

Your network needs to understand that messaging briefs have a shelf life and are reference documents not intended for wider distribution. If your public relations department is overly conservative, they may need assurance that you have a sophisticated team that knows how to use such briefs responsibly.

Communications is getting more diffused and crowd-sourced all the time. I'm happy to see the sun setting on a centralized, command-and-control approach, but message discipline has benefits. Remaining stingy with key messages and leaving your network in the dark, however, is risky. Without usable messaging, you're encouraging them to guess and create versions that don't mesh with global themes.

- **Clarity from corporate on intent:** Corporate communicators easily fall in love with their own creative work. They've been hashing it out for weeks with stakeholders, colleagues, and leadership. While that's going on, they'll warn their network that it's coming, but they won't show any work in progress. Why so secretive? Yes, it's still with people in legal, but they'll be sitting on it until the last minute. You can never talk too soon with your network about a campaign's proposed timing, intent, risks, and the creative choices that you're considering. Even if the campaign changes along the way, is never implemented, or the legal team changes the wording beyond all recognition, it's a learning opportunity. When the time comes to execute, your network will be better equipped if they know the background.
- **Insight into the what and why of the cutting room floor:** How many videos have we had to reject because there was an unacceptable *health and safety* practice in the background? Train those who take photos and create video about your company's sanctioned behaviors—policies such as driving with both hands on the wheel and holding handrails on stairs. They're likely to miss those details when they shoot, and if they do, health and safety managers will make you remove the visual. If specific videos or images are forbidden, make sure you conduct a *postmortem* with the entire network and cover lessons learned.
- **Immediate notification of surprises:** Your CEO had an idea in the shower and now the entire corporate team is racing to deliver. Even with surprises, don't forget to notify the global network of the possibility, the intent, the timeline, and what success might look like—everything you know at this point, even if it's murky. We all know that a sudden campaign may never get delivered, but the discussion will get your network thinking, give them advanced notice, and maybe even help you handle the campaign better. As Catmull writes, "Include people in your problems, not just your solutions"[10].
- **Let gurus embrace their status:** Local communicators should never be afraid to talk ideas over with Corporate Communications, but if you're in the early stages of developing a localization system, they might be. If they think of corporate as brand or messaging enforcers, they won't share anything until it's too late. However, if you build a collaborative relationship, they'll ask for advice while they're developing

ideas. Promote that habit, and they get an experienced perspective before they go on shoots or conduct interviews. Corporate gets advanced notice of local content that may be useful in other channels. Everybody wins.

- **Trust and give leeway to execute:** It's not easy to let go, especially given how often local content lacks strategic value. But you must. The quality of local output will get better with time if you constructively go over examples as a team. If you can't let go of the big pieces, give network members freedom to create content types that you believe have less risk (e.g., stories about local community involvement). Accountability for local messaging builds confidence, ownership, and skill sets.

Out in the field with my team, when I realize I forgot something important, I'm relieved to find out that they didn't. They become used to bringing the chargers, tripods, and *photo release* forms to every shoot. When they're solely responsible, communicators learn to check the background and lighting during photo shoots, screen out health and safety violations, and generally anticipate the many other things that can go wrong without needing to be reminded ahead of time.

- **Be someone to brag to:** People working on communications locally may be the only one with that responsibility in that market, and the business world can be stingy with praise for our kind. Be the person they want to tell when they get great results.
- **Tools and professional skills:** I once knew a human resources manager who brought his own expensive camera to an internal event to take photos. He promptly broke it and never offered the favor again. Most companies encourage the creation of video content for internal channels, but it's unfair to demand video if you don't provide equipment and video editing software. Don't ask your network to edit video on their personal computers. In fact, in some markets, it's illegal to ask. In addition to equipment and hardware, corporate bears responsibility for developing skills. If you want local communicators to keep up with new media, you have to hire talent who already have the skills, invest in professional development, or find money to outsource the work.

Developing general communications skills

Beyond developing content skills, you need to help your network master the profession's best practices. This is especially true if you have people who have come to the role from other disciplines. Depending on their backgrounds, you may have to build their communications skills from scratch. Here are a few ways to deepen their general knowledge.

- **Coach them to deflect low-value requests:** As Rosie Halfhead pointed out, network members can get bombarded with local requests for support. These demands are often for low-value tactics that depart from global communications strategy (e.g., they want a newsletter launched at the same time Corporate Communications is trying to build up a digital channel). If network members have only a loose relationship with corporate instead of a direct reporting line, those requests are outright orders.

  Communication pros are familiar with random requests like these, and they know how to qualify and prioritize them before taking action. But if your people are not fully dedicated to communications, they may not know how to ask qualifying questions or deflect low-priority requests for help. Teaching each communicator to assess requests and engage clients constructively is a key skill that will strengthen the network and the communications function across your business. The *Alive With Ideas*[2] blog has more on the conversation Communications needs to have with its clients.

- **Provide access to professional literature:** Most corporate training libraries are self-service educational properties, some offering thousands of courses online. But they have almost nothing that's relevant to the field of communications. You should consider funding access to industry best practice publications from sources such as Ragan,[3] Gartner,[4] or the International Association of Business Communicators (IABC).[5] Each offers in-depth research on best practices, some of which is free. Unfortunately, the best communication courses are expensive, and even

---

[3] https://www.ragan.com/about-us/
[4] https://www.gartner.com/en
[5] https://www.iabc.com/

when money isn't restricted, many people can't find time for training. If you can't afford paid memberships for development, it doesn't cost anything to talk about the reading you're doing on free platforms such as LinkedIn. Pointing out and discussing blog posts or research that you find interesting goes a long way toward boosting people's professional growth.

Sustaining global execution

Barbara Gibson advises communicators to continually develop intercultural competencies. "You often see teams giving up too soon, throwing up their hands in frustration because a specific tactic didn't work," she said in an interview.

International execution is like physical exercise. Going to the gym just a couple of times after New Year's won't change us much, but if we exercise every day and practice international awareness with every project, our efforts can be transformative. Here are four strategies to enable more international co-operation among your team and at headquarters:

- **Execute global rollouts in stages:** Abandon the simultaneous global launch whenever possible. Localization done right takes time, and in most instances, market-by-market rollouts will be fine. If you must have simultaneity, expand the project timeline to give your network a realistic amount of time to execute it well.
- **Job rotations and special projects:** Job rotations within the communications function at different locations can make headquarters practitioners more aware of the business, competitors in various markets, local conditions, and employee preferences. Organizationally, role rotations drive skills, adoption of tools, and best practices deeper into the business. If these placements are too expensive, consider creating special projects where communicators in various locations can work together virtually.
- **Show flexibility in style, tone, and subject matter:** American tone can have its charms, but its enthusiasm and willingness to self-promote leaves some cultures cold. People in cultures that value humility can be more reserved, and in another fallout from cultural bias, Amer-

icans often interpret unwillingness to participate as laziness or arrogance. A charismatic, high-energy leader may be able to successfully adapt Yankee-stylings, but you can't count on it happening everywhere or being interpreted consistently.

- **Train stakeholders in localization:** No matter the maturity of your localization program, keep your stakeholders and internal customers up to date on your practices and capabilities. When you get new team members, train them in localization expectations from the start. Even if they won't routinely be working with translations, they should understand the process.

When you design programs whose success depends on others' participation (e.g., when you count on user-generated content), remember that many will be hesitant to volunteer. They might, however, be persuaded with a little local support. Global campaigns and goal setting are full of incorrect assumptions, so involve the network in project design to improve the chances for success.

CHAPTER 16
Working with Your Network

In a perfect world, your company would have competent, English-speaking communications professionals in each market. In practice, most companies view such resources as too expensive, especially for smaller markets.

Having the mandate and budget to expand a communications function in every country would be nice, but it's not something most companies are willing to do.

That doesn't mean you can't improve. It doesn't cost money for the corporate office to develop an international mindset, and training your existing network doesn't have to be expensive—though it may take some time to motivate business units to support it with people who don't report to you.

No matter your network's maturity, you can build on what you have. Training a network and developing them falls naturally to the communications function, since corporate learning and development programs rarely focus on these skills.

It's important to recognize that not everyone is cut out for a career in communications. Just because local management has assigned someone to the job, that doesn't mean they're suited to it or even want it. Until you can convince leadership that you need better resources, you may be stuck with people in local business units who think an email or a poster is enough to solve a business problem.

> If you're starting from scratch, it will take time to build communications skills.

One client, a mid-sized global manufacturer, had recently rolled out a new name and logo. As part of the roll out, a branding agency created attractive, detailed design guidelines that described how to use visual elements of the brand identity.

When it came to images, they called for live-action, real-life photos. They placed big red Xs on staged, posed photos of smiling models and artificial scenes of plastic water bottles flying in the sky.

Immediately after the brand rollout, the first article the internal communications team posted on their intranet was about preventing phishing attacks. They chose two photos: a stock photo of a fishhook on a keyboard, and a faceless figure in a hoodie hovering ominously over a monitor. When I pointed out that these were off brand, the author and the communications director, intelligent and capable people, looked at me as if I'd asked them to continue the meeting in Klingon.[1]

"Well how else do you depict cyber security?" they asked.

I didn't have an answer, and I can sympathize with both sides. The brand strategists want us to avoid overused, cliché images, but on the practitioner side, finding useful, memorable photos can take ages. (Note to branding consultants: good, real-life photography isn't easy to get).

What I remember most about that conversation is the reaction of those two communicators. Even where the guidelines and best practices are explicit and freshly launched, the daily reality of creating on-brand content can be tough, even at headquarters. It's especially tough for those working on their own with limited time and money.

To build a strong network, more experienced communicators should provide frequent guidance in the day-to-day choices local communicators make. Those choices may be cultural, but there may also be better options they weren't aware of.

Thinking like a communicator

Improving your network's skills depends on the maturity of your localization program, what resources local countries bring to the table, and the amount of time and energy you can spend.

---

[1] Klingon [https://www.kli.org/] is a fictional language from the *Star Trek* television series. It has attracted many learners over the years, and Duolingo offers a course in Klingon.

Corporate's resources are likely to be the most experienced in spotting, shaping, and telling stories, but not everyone in the network needs a specialized degree. I've met good communicators from other fields, and you can certainly improve the skills of anyone who is motivated to learn. It's relatively easy to teach people to size a photo or work with your content management system. But it's hard to get people to write with an audience in mind. Business people often confuse communicating with informing, and telling stories with emotional elements just doesn't occur to them.

When local business units report on an event, they provide only a few factual statements (i.e., the where and when but not the what and the why). They may identify people in photos selectively, with captions pointing out only executives, leaving the peasants anonymous. In presentations and white papers, they provide facts, seemingly all of them, expecting those facts to speak for themselves. They assume their readers are with them for every word, no matter the length, and conclude with a sentence that would better serve as their lead.

Corporate requests for local storytelling often go unfulfilled. When you get them, you may find they're missing opportunities to reinforce direction and strategy.

> Many business people wouldn't know a good story if you read it to them at bedtime.

To better understand the potential of local resources, have frequent conversations with the people in your network about content. Brainstorm with them variations on how to structure stories, what visual assets they should pursue, and how they should go about leveraging the content after it's published.

If you can inspire them to come to you for advice early enough, you can help with content and show them how to use key messages. When the network trusts its global support and can demonstrate competence, corporate's role shifts from pushing content down to the countries to empowering and enabling creativity. To get your network routinely developing strategic content on their own without waiting for marching orders, you must continually discuss their work with them in a collaborative context.

Maintaining a dialogue about tone

Your brand guidelines probably have a few paragraphs on tone and voice. You should use those paragraphs as a starting place to talk about tone and voice with your network.

If guidelines cover the brand's voice, they will typically describe writing that is personal, friendly, human, and free of jargon. I'd be all for that, and if a company is able to achieve it, it could be strongly differentiating.

But achieving that kind of writing isn't easy, even in one language. Writing with a direct and clear voice can be a struggle for people outside of communications. Unless they've spent time learning how to revise writing and how to move toward plain language, most business writing will be dense first drafts, full of specialized terms and stilted, ambiguous abstractions.

Jargon is universally reviled. When I defined it in a blog post, it became my most popular post to date.[2] People use the word *jargon* with obvious distaste, but they don't necessarily recognize jargon in their own work. While their terms are clear to them, they don't appreciate that people outside their sphere won't take the time to decipher them. Unfortunately, some of the people in your network may suffer from this same skills gap.

The topic of tone and voice is a way to discuss writing in languages that you don't speak. Global communications is a minefield when it comes to matters of tone, and discussing the intent of writing is a way to navigate it.

Not every aspect of your brand's tone will translate into each culture. If your brand guidelines are to be friendly, discuss regularly with your co-creators what the intention behind that friendliness is. Friendly may not be appropriate in some cultures, but you may be able to work around this. For example, if your company emphasizes a friendly tone because it wants customers to associate the brand with attentiveness and quick response, discuss this with your network. They may be able make an adjustment and strike a tone that works within their culture.

---

[2] "Jargon: Another Chance to Make it About You."[60].

Corporate can badly miss, and inexperienced local staff may adopt a cheerful tone for more serious news.[3] Discuss your network member's tone choices before they create content, and don't forget to also cover the tone of graphics, photos, videos, audio, and live events. Through these discussions, you will also learn more about the topics they choose to cover, the way they go about building content, and the key messages they use.

Encouraging honest discussion

People from content backgrounds expect teamwork, but it may be new to people who started in other fields. One-on-one meetings are good for involving local staff in content planning. As teaching moments come up, discuss them as a group.

Discuss with your network the hits and misses of the team at headquarters to demonstrate that communications don't come tumbling down from a mountaintop. Deliverables are created by people, and those people can have differences of opinion. These conversations show your team respect, bring them into the process, and demonstrate the critical thinking they need in order to advance as communications professionals. The discussion keeps strategy top of mind and builds consensus on how communicators should think.

> It's especially important that corporate hold its own work up to scrutiny.

Mentoring communicators

In distributed, virtual teams, bonding can be superficial. A mentoring program can help strengthen a person's bond with colleagues and with the profession. Anna Schlegel,[4] vice president of global portfolio-to-market lifecycle at NetApp, is a co-founder of Women in Localization,[5] a global community for the advancement of women and the localization industry.

---

[3] I've seen email drafts meant to notify specific employees that they would be expected to train their replacements that were full of exclamation points, looking forward to a bright future with fewer people.

[4] Anna Schlegel is the author of *Truly Global: The Theory and Practice of Bringing Your Company to International Markets*[45]. Her book focuses on localization practices for customers, but anyone building localization teams for employee communications can learn from it.

[5] https://womeninlocalization.com/

Your network will certainly have people who can benefit from membership. Among its many efforts to share best practice, it offers a mentor matchmaking service.

Schlegel frequently speaks on mentoring. She has a 13-minute presentation, "Grow Your Localization Career with Mentoring"[46], that gives good advice for people on both sides of the mentoring relationship.

Getting the network in touch with the business

Complaints that corporate communicators are out of touch are common, but the same can often be said of the network. If their time is spent in a single office, they're not exactly hands-on with the business either.

Encourage your network to establish contacts at every level in their local business units. The network should regularly arrange site visits, ride alongs, and face-time with local leadership. These contacts will give them input for content; site visits almost always result in at least one good piece of content, and the personal contacts are valuable over time.

The entire communications function stands to benefit from interactions with business units in several other ways:

- Local business people get acquainted with your network.
- Local staff become more apt to share.
- Your network learns about pain points it can help address.
- Your network unearths photos and other assets for content.

In some settings, leaders won't consider a communications person important enough to warrant meetings. If politics and local class differences make it difficult to request meetings directly, a communications manager might need to request time on their behalf, help with the arrangements, and possibly participate.

Don't cascade; drive a message

Organizations put a lot of faith in cascading information. Unfortunately information isn't water; it needs a little help to flow, and your network can provide that help. Your network can use corporate backgrounders to create localized briefings for global campaigns. Make sure your network knows how to adapt content so that managers can use it in face-to-face meetings.

These local briefings can build relationships and demonstrate the power of our profession first-hand. You can empower your network to provide value locally and drive greater penetration of strategic messaging.

Content development that builds relationships

The best content is built collaboratively. Here are some practices that can help your network create better content and improve relations between corporate and local networks.

- **Maintain a calendar of yearly events:** There are company-wide events that are predictable from year to year or that are planned out months in advance. Maybe it's an annual celebration, a release of commissioned research, sponsored content, a product that will premiere at a trade fair, a recognition event, or compulsory training. Make sure the network knows these milestones in advance, and start brainstorming assets and tactics with them early. In content meetings, discuss their milestones and annual events and decide whether content about it might be interesting to audiences outside that country.
- **Holidays:** Religious holidays like Christmas and Easter are touchy in global communication channels. Content that leans heavily on religious holidays is not necessarily global.

  A company's brand can be part of holiday cheer—if we learn how to make appropriate creative use of it. The occurrence of religious holidays is predictable, so you can look ahead and create assets that local business units will want to use. Don't assume that local holiday content is always better. Many people see their home culture as more homogenous than it really is. Corporate may in fact be more tuned into issues of global diversity than the network or local managers, so do what you can to make sure your local businesses don't create insensitive material.

- **Commemorative days:** Too often we learn about these days too late. It's disheartening to see other companies ready with social media posts on a topic relevant to your global message when you are days away from assembling something worthwhile. Your network can help you with this if you anticipate UN commemorative days together and discuss possibilities ahead of time.
- **Local holidays:** Romanian colleagues once sent me a photo of a local office celebration. They wanted me to post it immediately to our intranet, thinking it would be compelling for employees worldwide. Anybody who's worked in internal communications will be familiar with this kind of request.

The photo wasn't compelling. It was another image of people posing with cake, a classic local babies-and-birthdays subject with no appeal to those who don't know the people in the picture.

When I dug a little deeper, I learned they were marking a traditional celebration, one that's something like Valentine's Day and unique to Romania. Already it was more interesting than the "today we had cake" angle, but there wasn't enough time to develop it for a regional or global story. So I noted it in the following year's calendar.

You can work with your network to anticipate their celebrations and discuss with them how local and global versions of this type of content might look. They will appreciate the help, and you may be able to use their content more broadly.

- **A collegial review of content in progress:** More than anything, corporate and local teams will work better when they brainstorm together, before the interviews are completed, before the photos get taken, and before it's too late for a re-write. It should feel routine to talk tactics and key messages together. A newsroom meeting or a SCRUM is better than an impersonal status report.

Team purpose and postmortems

Jonathan Phillips told me that a *postmortem*—an honest peer-to-peer discussions about successes and failures at the conclusion of a project—is an essential part of feedback for communicators. "If we do not take the time to assess the performance of our work—that is to say, the outcomes—then we will fail to learn and fail to get better. Postmortems should be rigorous and include the project costs and employee time spent to produce the work. We need to be more scientific and understand the cost and value," he said. "I also support postmortems being completed by teams outside of comms to provide a truly objective summary. We should not mark our own homework."

In the "Broadening Our View" chapter in *Creativity, Inc.*, Ed Catmull describes a postmortem as an all-hands-on-deck meeting after the completion of a movie where they discuss the good and the bad.

He writes that postmortems:

- Consolidate what's been learned
- Teach others who weren't there
- Prevent resentment from festering
- Force reflection
- Raise questions that should be asked during the next project

These are good goals for employee communication networks too. He admits postmortems range from profoundly helpful to a waste of time, but he says the spirit of the meeting is its true value, where honesty is expected and people feel no risk of retribution. He provides a few ways to vary the structure of such meetings to encourage more candor and fresh insight. The entire chapter is a useful read for any creative manager.

Catmull outlines other useful possibilities that creative teams should consider. They include encouraging experimentation, leading research trips, and solving problems together.

Content that both corporate and local communicators get wrong

Community involvement

The boom in reporting on *corporate social responsibility (CSR)* means that private and public companies of all sizes want to demonstrate they're good citizens. To document CSR, corporations want more evidence of local involvement in the communities where they operate. Year round, corporate looks for content on community engagement to include in their annual report and to earn likes in social media.

For communicators, reporting on community involvement has frustrations. Interpretations of community involvement vary. For communicators, coming up with a storyline that unifies local CSR activity is a challenge.

At the same time, headquarters might not give global coverage or offer matching funds to some activities. Some corporate purses won't open for charities that help the homeless, AIDS patients, or refugees, preferring feel-good, photogenic causes with kids, tree planting, and beach cleanups.

Employees hear expressions like "make a difference" and want to pitch in where they see the greatest local need. But if their support for a particular cause, say refugee relief, somehow doesn't count to corporate, they get discouraged from participating.

In the US, neighborhood activities are easy for corporations to find and fund. In Europe, taxes are high and most social services are better provided for. At the same time, the planning and permissions required to take pictures in a European city during a park cleanup can be a deal killer. In Asia, community involvement can be a local office making a donation. I once saw a story from a South Korean business unit about financial support for a market of local artisans. They saw it as community engagement, while corporate was confused because it wasn't a formal, recognized charity.

Americans see calls for corporate-sanctioned volunteering or fundraising as normal, while Europeans regularly complain about them. One business unit for a European client supported a local school, and people joked about how often the classrooms needed paint. Some people like teams and rallying behind colors, but not everyone is willing to put on a baseball cap or be photographed in matching T-shirts.

Inspiring Europeans to get involved in community can be done, but the appeal should be in a way that's in tune with their values, and this is where your network can be valuable.

Employee recognition

Recognition is a term human resources, management, and communications departments use to describe the formal celebration of outstanding efforts ("Let's give a round of applause to these two!").

Recognition is said to be psychologically motivating and empowering. Given those positive feelings, you'd think it would be easy to find internal stories to develop into content, but it's not. The thorniness of recognition schemes outside the US can be especially hard for Americans to grasp.

I've heard several European variations on the expression, "the tallest flower gets cut." In some cultures it doesn't pay to stand out, and people will be reluctant to share a story that touts their own success.

Pride in the company is another area of cultural misunderstanding. Americans routinely say they're proud of their company, while Europeans find this bizarre and cultish. So when corporate asks for employee quotes about what makes them proud about working for this company, they get nothing. That in turn frustrates US colleagues and makes them think that Europeans are gloomy and sour.

Maybe both have a point, but reframing the request even slightly can generate more usable reactions. Get people to talk about their connection to the work, not the company. Ask them if they admire their colleagues, if they feel satisfaction in the work they do, or if they're happy with the outcome of a certain project, and you will get a reaction much closer to what you originally hoped for.

This kind of storytelling content is easier for the local network to gather. They can ensure the question is posed correctly, and it will empower them as the local communicator. They'll know what kind of photos, quotes, and permission forms to gather. They'll get better input than if you have a central, global collection point.

One word of caution: local doesn't always mean authentic. Corporate's clamoring for volunteering or recognition pieces can be a cultural bias in itself. I once had a local communicator on our team who was a rising star in the eyes of corporate, thanks to his local-language videos. We later learned that he gave his video subjects a script. He crafted his videos to be popular with corporate, which they were, and they were widely distributed to global audiences. But I doubt these videos had much credibility on location. It felt as though we'd encouraged him to create a Potemkin village.[6] Developing a network built on trust and frequent collaboration should help prevent such misguided efforts.

Health and Safety (H&S)

Almost every industrial workplace tells its employees that H&S is a top priority. To prove it, Corporate Communications produces posters, content, and campaigns to remind people about safe practices. Local managers follow suit and produce their own versions of the same message.

> Whether it's from corporate or from local management, H&S content is rarely effective.

Many business people have complete faith that the only reason accidents happen is a lack of awareness, so they keep rolling out posters, content, and campaigns. But communications deliverables have little impact on safety performance. Employees in operations already know they're supposed to wear gloves, and reminders feel condescending.

A UK-based expert in H&S, now a senior communications consultant, told me that during his years in industrial operations, he saw several companies

---

[6] A Potemkin village is anything built to convey the impression that things are better than they really are. The term comes from Grigory Potemkin, who supposedly built a mobile false village to fool Russian Empress Catherine II into thinking conditions in the Crimea where better than they were (https://en.wikipedia.org/wiki/Potemkin_village).

transform their safety performance for the better. But he said that that none of them did it with posters. "Focusing on safety has to go all through the organization. In Communications, we have a central edict to reduce accidents, and we expect managers to support that. My view is that it should be the other way around."

If companies would think about driving performance instead of awareness, they'd do more than issue reminders. "Companies must create a culture where employees are encouraged to speak out when things go wrong. Context and leadership are important. Extravagant communications about your number-one priority are not," he said.

He conceded that communications can contribute positively. "There is definitely a role for communications, and if you get it right it can be fantastic. But it can't be a substitute for management intervention. What we see from corporate is often irrelevant, distant, and incongruent from the way things are happening at the line level. If it can be made relevant, congruent, and emotional, it can be powerful, but I don't see many organizations doing that. They tick boxes and send posters."

He added that the most recent ISO standard on occupational health and safety, *ISO 45001*,[7] now has less content about standard procedures and more about leadership and culture. "From safety to quality to performance management, there is a great deal of innovative thinking out there. Sadly for the creative industry, Communications is lagging."

---

[7] *Occupational health and safety, ISO 45001*[24].

CHAPTER 17
Developing Your Network

"It's nice to finally put a face with the name."

We're used to virtual relationships by now, but it's no mystery that it's easier to get to know colleagues in person. Bringing your network into the same place periodically can unify your shared sense of purpose, increase job satisfaction and build skills. But when you're fortunate to get approval for such an expense, you're wasting a huge opportunity if you use a conventional team-meeting format.

In other words, ditch the PowerPoint.

It doesn't help to put everyone in a darkened room for an entire day talking about what corporate needs from them, punctuated by short breaks where everyone goes off and responds to email from home. Nobody will get much from the expense and the bother. You might as well have a conference call.

You and your network need to interact with and learn from each other. Even if you must present corporate PowerPoint decks about global strategy, build in plenty of unstructured networking time.

It's important that Corporate Communications show how to create content rather than tell. Don't engineer stuff for the network to consume at a meeting. Don't waste time going over templates, processes, and form filling. They can do those things on their own time. When you are together, treat your network like the creatives they are (or that you wish them to be). Talk one-on-one, meet as smaller teams, and facilitate workshops.

Group meetings

I'm not huge a fan of the weekly, compulsory department meeting. Is anyone? They become a roll call where people feel obligated to list what's keeping them busy. Not only is it a time killer, I've always found such meetings demotivating, as if we're not trusted to prioritize work.

Of course content managers want to have some idea of what people are working on so that they can plan and optimize their editorial calendar. But rather than cover everyone's activities on a team call, talk one-on-one with them about content they're working on. A one-on-one is an opportunity to brainstorm various approaches and reduces the sense that they're in competition with other team members. If you're in the US, one-on-ones are better for your network in Asia. Because of time differences, regular group meetings are likely in their late evening, but one-on-ones can be scheduled at times that are more comfortable for them.

If you discuss content as a group, cover only content that all participants have a chance to see (i.e., leave the headquarters, home-country content out of the meeting). When you talk about upcoming global content, ask your network if they have local examples that dovetail with the global message. Help them brainstorm stories and decide together what channels could use their stories. Involve as many people as possible in posing questions and proposing solutions. The purpose of covering these topics isn't to check their work, it's to get them sharing ideas.

Network members have varying levels of experience and dedication. Major-market members may be more experienced and could dominate an all-hands meeting. Network meetings should be segmented into smaller groups based on the level of resources in each market. Agile SCRUM meetings[1] can be a productive way to organize editorial working sessions. With a short, daily check-in and continual re-assessment of plans, a SCRUM format could be a good way to uncover creative assets that can be shared or initiatives that can be connected to content.

Examples of smaller group meetings could include the following:

- Major-market communicators
- Mid-market communicators
- Smaller countries giving Communications only part of their work week
- Corporate content creators

---

[1] See Michael Lum's article, "5 Scrum Meeting Best Practices: Master the Daily Stand-Up"[33], for some tips on handling this kind of meeting.

These smaller-group meetings help keep everyone aware of assets appropriate to their needs and uncover barriers in common that corporate can work to remove. Corporate SCRUMs can focus on international needs for content that's going to be shared outside the home country. SCRUMs of all creators within a region are more likely to work in the same time zone, and the assets they share are probably more culturally usable in their work. That is, even if a photo was obviously taken in Italy, it could still be more useful to audiences in Germany than a photo from Detroit.

More than status reports, these are working sessions where you look together at specific examples of global and local work. Hopefully, corporate will take some criticism. Discussing criticism openly demonstrates to less-than-confident members that they can speak up if they think something won't work, and it encourages them to take a more active role in shaping content. Participants in network meetings should understand that they have a stake and are not just order takers waiting for direction from corporate.

> **Practical Tip: Include translators in editorial meetings**
> If you have translators, include them in editorial meetings occasionally. Translators will benefit from knowing more about your process, your priorities, the purpose of a specific piece, the timing, and the messaging. This background will inform the tone choices they make in their translations and make them more confident when they're working in isolation and on a tight deadline.

What to do in skills workshops

Every company I've worked for has a large catalog of online courses, but very little of it is relevant to communicators. Our skills and aspirations are unusual in the business world.

Corporate Communications should be a hub for professional development. Collaborative workshops are a great way to network, learn from each other, instill confidence, and address your team's development needs.

In workshops, team members can work in small groups to maximize participation. The headquarters team and more experienced communicators should circulate, listening in and facilitating where needed.

Workshops can be organized around practical, day-to-day tasks. In just a couple of hours, big improvements can be achieved on topics such as:

- Storytelling
- Producing effective video with phones
- Photography best practices and legal considerations
- Staying brand compliant using templates and Microsoft Office tools

The content you discuss has to be translated into a shared language, but you probably don't need a high-quality translation. You should be able to get by with a quick and free machine translation, such as Google Translate.

Discussing work critically won't be easy at first. They're probably not used to looking at their work so closely, especially in another language. Work to keep groups small to maximize each network member's participation and talking time.

Here are some of the workshop topics you can organize:

- **Good and not-so-good recent examples:** Was a piece of content a success? What were the alternatives and what impact might they have had? Can the story be repurposed, revisited or expanded in future content? Would other locations find it interesting? Can you create complementary pieces from other locations?
- **Global and local content that's in development:** Explore the process of content creation. Determine the objective, the target audience, what success measures it might contribute to, and key messages. Go over the risks (i.e., What happens if it's ignored? What happens if it's not?). Brainstorm alternative approaches and discuss how local versions might differ.

- **Measurement workshops:** Communications measurement is likely something that local businesses have never done before. A workshop on measurement deepens skills and gets them thinking. Rather than assigning metrics that are meaningful only to corporate, find out what your network thinks should be measured.
- **Shared objectives and strategy:** Discuss the pros and cons of global communications goals. For example, if you want communications to be more visual, or if you want priorities shifted to new channels, you can discuss with the network whether they agree and what they can do to enable new approaches.

> Practical Tip: Conduct annual measurement workshops
>
> For all its variation, the good news about operating in multiple countries is that you have opportunity to target, experiment, and measure.
>
> In Chapter 2, I outlined why it's often impossible to make valid comparisons country to country. Think instead about comparing similar business units and countries with a similar demographic makeup (i.e., wired versus non-wired employees, generational makeup, percent of employees originally hired by a legacy company, etc.).
>
> To determine which comparisons will be meaningful, let the network help. Give team members access to measurement tools, train them in using them, encourage them to seek comparisons and to partner with their local human resources to look at demographics. Discuss results with them. It's an opportunity to better target communications, draw unique conclusions, and define your company's own best practice.
>
> A workshop where you discuss content categories to measure can also help them tune digital skills to business needs. Look for balance: too many categories and no one uses them, too few and your results are not calibrated to priorities.
>
> If your company has goal setting as an annual ritual, have measurement workshops in time for people to incorporate goals and results in their performance plan.

Values-driven workshops

Ed Catmull explains how management style can either support or detract from the values a company wants to foster:

> "The silver lining of a major meltdown is that it gives managers a chance to send clear signals to employees about the company's values, which inform the role each individual should expect to play. When we respond to the flaws of a movie in development by throwing it out and restarting, we are telling people that we value the quality of our movies more than anything else."
>
> —Ed Catmull, *Creativity, Inc.*[10]

Every network interaction has this potential. You can say the words innovate, collaborate, and co-operate and claim to be anti-hierarchical, but interacting with your network is where you put these concepts into practice.

Before your localization program, they may have only evaluated the volume of their output. Catmull writes that it takes time for any group to develop the trust to speak candidly, but the success of your future creative projects depends on it.

Collaborating through problems

> "Include people in your problems, not just your solutions." Ed Catmull, *Creativity, Inc.*[10]

Surprises and problems continually come up for communicators at headquarters, and when they do, the network should be brought into the discussion. Problems are an important area for collaboration and mutual learning. Their proximity to local business units will help you make more informed choices, and they'll learn more about conditions driving global strategy.

One example of corporate and local co-operation is navigating Europe's *works councils*. European countries require large companies to maintain councils, made up of employees, who review programs or changes that affect employee experience. Companies operating in European Union countries are additionally required to maintain a European-level, multi-country works council.[2]

The structure and powers of these works councils vary, and union-averse American companies often confuse works councils with unions. US managers can get frustrated when a works council review slows down a global initiative, and they often see works councils as adversaries.

Works councils rarely have complete veto power, but to get a hearing, they do need advanced notice. Depending on their meeting schedule, it can take several weeks. It took one client more than a year to get approval from its German works council to allow employees in that country to access *Workplace by Facebook*.

The relationship doesn't have to be adversarial. To Communications, works council members are influencers among the employee population and therefore potential allies. Human resources or labor usually manages the relationship, but the communications network should be aware of the meeting schedule and the tone of the relationship. Communications should contribute to meeting agendas and participate if invited.

Get a second opinion

On most issues, I defer to the judgment of local staff. But they also have biases. Getting acquainted with them personally helps you gauge what you hear from them.

Their interests and what they are willing to execute can skew their beliefs about what their fellow employees will or won't accept. The people who told me that programs dreamed up at headquarters would never work also told me that employees would never log on to an online platform, would never follow the company on social media, and would never check for company information on their own devices. Over time, experience proved otherwise.

---

[2] See "European Works Councils"[19] for more on works councils in Europe.

> In each country, have an avenue to get a second opinion. If you leave yourself with just one contact in a market, what you produce will reflect that person's tastes.

I once saw a client's Europe region marketing team opt-out of a corporate Christmas holiday campaign. Although the European business was starved for advertising budget, they rejected the campaign because they thought it sentimental and stereotypically American. (I had no say in the decision, but I agreed with them.) Because of this, the content was promoted only in US social media. When the campaign went viral worldwide, European locations missed out on fully leveraging the content.

Audiences are unpredictable. You shouldn't give up trying to develop global content just because local network members don't think it will work, don't like collecting examples, or do a poor job with execution. An ongoing, thoughtful discussion gives you a chance to push back on entrenched, negative beliefs about what's possible.

Career development for creative teams

The communication department's mission may not match that of people in the network. Ask them frequently what they want. Talk with them about what they need and discuss prospects for making that happen. You must learn what motivates them to do good work, what they like doing, and what they aspire to.

Having these conversations regularly—more often than the traditional annual review—will also tell them more about who you are, what you're hoping for, and whether they can see a future with you.

> Getting to know your network personally is how you learn that, outside of work, members organize art exhibitions, take classes in XML, or want to start editing video. You won't know until you get acquainted.

For professional development, you can't just leave your team to forage on their own. Share with them reading and webinars that you find useful and encourage them to do the same.

High-quality development resources are routinely available from organizations like The Content Wrangler, Content Rules, Alive With Ideas, Center for Plain Language, Institute of Internal Communications (IoIC), Precision Content, Localization Institute, Ragan Communications, Gartner, Poppulo, Bananatag, Happeo, and more. Take the opportunity to discuss best practices and why they would or wouldn't work in your organization. The more you involve your network, the more you can expect from them.

Part IV Conclusion

Maintaining global capabilities in communications requires ongoing maintenance of skills, a flexible mindset, and a willingness to change. International practices vary across locations, but they don't have to be expensive. You'll probably invest more in your strategic markets, but no matter where you implement localization or at what level, as you cultivate more skills and develop best practices, more and more will be expected. Where localization takes root, especially in larger, more resourced markets, there will be an evolution toward co-creation.

CHAPTER 18
Afterword

"I don't share any of that."

"To be honest, sometimes I don't understand it."

"Headquarters is good at broadcasting, less good at listening."

I began this book knowing that English-only puts a significant limit on the effectiveness of our communications. In doing the research and talking to experts from other fields, I'm convinced more than ever that internal, global deliverables as they're conventionally created have hardly any traction. As good as their English is, people are busy.

> Messages that don't speak their language or that don't reflect their daily work experience are just going to be ignored or glanced at and forgotten.

It's not getting any easier, and the conditions global companies operate in are even more complex than is commonly understood. When we think about language and geography, we conflate political and linguistic boundaries: German language in Germany or Spanish in Spain. We picture the US as an English-speaking country with pockets of immigrant communities. History is messier than that, and such a simplified view is particularly inaccurate in an age of digital communication and job mobility.

I've seen workplace notices posted in Chicago in English, Spanish, and Polish. German cities have long-established Turkish communities and Polish shops catering to transplants. Every language of the world seems to be spoken in London, and in my current home of Prague, government offices sometimes provide services in Vietnamese and Russian. Globalization is on every corner.

I wrote this book because corporate communication departments are stuck in the past, complacent in the belief that English is the global language and that employees everywhere get the message.

Throughout my career I've been focused on content, but almost all of it was for destination intranets—the kind that people have to seek out and maybe even log on to. Whenever I talk to users about what kind of content they're interested in, they tell me that they visit the company intranet only when they need to access something for work tasks. It's been this way for a long time, and measurement shows they're telling the truth.

The content we publish on our intranets about company strategy and news has always been important, but it's evidently not a big enough draw. Except for sites that deliver information that employees need daily, few people find their way to our content. An analogy one consultant told me was that he reads ads on the subway, but he doesn't take the subway to read ads.

In a newly emerging media environment, our content may become even more irrelevant. After years of being bound to platforms, applications, and fixed server locations, companies are moving to cloud-based systems and hybrids that can provide employees with more personalized service.

Digital-enabled collaboration is happening in spaces that those of us in Communications don't influence, let alone control. Human resources forums are talking about delivering consumer-like experiences on internal platforms. Users post content on *Yammer* and *Workplace by Facebook* in any language they choose (both claim to support more than 100 languages).

These changes will continue to accelerate. Cloud computing, artificial intelligence, machine learning and automated translation are going to evolve individuals' relationships with their organizations.

> Our channels, systems, and tools are increasingly ready for the multilingual world, but we in Communications may not be ready for it.

The processes and resources we use to communicate with employees are as centralized as ever. Our intranet content management systems already support multiple languages, but we don't use them.

Adapting company communications to new realities will take much more than figuring out translation processes. If we expect people to consume content, it must be in their preferred language, easy on the eye, available on the device of their choice, and relevant to their business unit and location.

Making this transition will not be easy for Corporate Communications. We must start thinking differently and develop new skills. Instead of lumbering along with old models, the communications function needs to rethink how to earn a seat at the table and, in fact, where to find the table. We have to think less about how to strengthen our chief executive's on-camera presence and more about how to strengthen the communications of line-level managers. We must worry less about content creation and more about how we enable quality content that's created and delivered locally.

People's expectations for local content are only going to intensify. They'll want Turkish content in Hamburg and Polish content in Chicago. To meet that demand, we're going to have to look ahead to a day when each market offers content in all the languages spoken by employees there.

Managing multiple versions and maintaining content accuracy will be complex, so we have to start thinking about what the terms global and local mean for our organizations. How is this content going to be delivered, and what resources can make it happen?

We must break out of the old-fashioned, we send/you receive model. Translating is a good first step, but it's not going to be enough. No two localization processes look alike, and we have to learn to co-create. We must develop skilled practitioners and learn to trust them.

No matter what digital transformation has in store for us, success or failure in communications will depend on a human connection. Learning more about our local communicators has never been more urgent.

It's time we got to know them.

APPENDIX A
Interviewee Biographies

Arlene Birt
Arlene is founder and chief visual storyteller at Background Stories, an information design consultancy that works with organizations in the US, EU, and UK to translate complex ideas, systems, and metrics into clear visuals that help people understand sustainability. Since 2008, Arlene has been a public artist and professor at the Minneapolis College of Art and Design, teaching courses on infodesign, data visualization, and sustainability.

Deborah S. Bosley
Dr. Deborah S. Bosley is owner and principal in The Plain Language Group. She also is professor emeritus of English (Technical Communication) at UNC Charlotte. As an international expert in the use of plain language, she has spent the past twenty years working in regulatory environments helping attorneys, corporations, government agencies, and non-profits create written information that exceeds compliance standards and that's easy for people to understand and use.

Dr. Barbara Gibson
Barbara is the principal of Cultural Resolution, a global business consultancy focused on helping companies that operate internationally achieve greater success when working across cultures. She is a lecturer in intercultural business communication at a number of universities and business schools in the UK and around the world.

Rosie Halfhead
Rosie is the founder of R-Co, a niche consultancy working internationally with start-ups, privately owned companies, and non-profits across a range of sectors on strategy and brand, marketing and sales, and stakeholder engagement and loyalty. She has broad international and multicultural exper-

ience in the B2B sector, having lived and worked in Belgium, Hong Kong, and the UK. Rosie is a former member of the executive committee of SWIFT, a global financial messaging provider, and she is an advisory board member of Echo, experts in communication, brand, and reputation research.

John Kohl

John is the author of *The Global English Style Guide: Writing Clear, Translatable Documentation for a Global Market*[28], widely recognized as the clearest and most extensive set of sentence- and phrase-level guidelines for writing for global audiences. John worked at SAS Institute as a technical writer, technical editor, and linguistic engineer for 25 years before retiring in 2017. As a linguistic engineer, he customized and supported Acrolinx software, as well as other tools and processes that helped make SAS documentation more consistent, easier to translate, and easier for non-native speakers of English to understand.

Prof. Élise LeMoing Maas

Élise is head of the public relations department at the Institut des Hautes Études des Communications Sociales (IHECS) in Brussels. After twenty years of experience in communications agencies and international companies, she now focuses on teaching and research in organizational communication at a number of universities in France, Belgium, Morocco, and Canada. She is also a communications consultant with Ganéos SPRL.

Sean Matthews

Sean is president and CEO of Visix, Inc., a provider of digital signage software, content designs, and meeting room signs, headquartered in Atlanta, US. He has over thirty years of sales and marketing experience in the audiovisual and digital signage industries. Sean is a graduate of the College of Charleston and Georgia State University. He served in the United States Marine Corps and the Marine Corps Reserve between 1985 and 1992.

Interviewee Biographies   213

Gerry McGovern

Gerry helps large organizations deliver a better digital customer experience. Gerry has developed Top Tasks, a customer experience management model, as a result of fifteen years of research and experience. Top Tasks is a research and management model that helps organizations improve customer experience through identifying and optimizing customer top tasks.

A highly regarded speaker, he has spoken on digital customer experience in more than thirty-five countries. He has written seven books on digital customer experience. His latest is called *Top Tasks*, which is a detailed how-to implementation guide.

Mark Ohlsen

Mark is the owner of LRS Recording, a specialist in foreign language media production. LRS has 35 years of experience working with more than 130 video production companies, translation companies and A/V departments of Fortune 100 and Fortune 500 companies. LRS was founded on the idea of helping business decision makers expand their ability to reach across language barriers with successful media localization training and campaigns.

Alan Oram

Alan is a co-founder of Alive With Ideas, a creative agency in the UK that blogs frequently on employee communications. With over twenty years' experience in creative communications for organizations of all shapes and sizes, he is on a mission to make work a better place to be through great communication. He supports the comms community with initiatives that shape understanding of the needs of employees and more broadly the constantly evolving workplace.

Jonathan Phillips

Jonathan is a co-founder at Lithos Partners and an independent digital strategy consultant, focusing on communication, collaboration, and digital workplace technologies. With twenty years' blue-chip experience, he is a regular keynote speaker, a contributor to the digital community, and a recognized global expert. He is a communication advisor to the UK government and the University of Bristol, charity chairman, non-exec director, and co-founder of Intranetizen.com.

Alan J. Porter

Alan is driven to educate, inform, and entertain through content. He is an industry leading content strategist, author of *The Content Pool*[70] and *WIKI*, and a regular conference speaker, workshop leader, and writer on content marketing, content strategy, customer experience, brand management, and content and localization strategy. In 2016 and 2017, MindTouch named Alan as one of the Top 25 Content Strategy Influencers, and CMSWire named him a Digital Strategy thought leader.

Leonard Rau

Leonard has been helping clients author and implement a winning brand strategy for more than twenty years in partnership with corporate communications agencies. He is a brand and marketing leader with extensive integrated marketing and multi-channel experience working across advertising, retail, brand, internal, corporate communication, and B2B and B2C sales activation projects. Leonard's work balances customer desires with the needs of the business.

Ann Rockley

Ann Rockley is CEO of The Rockley Group, Inc. She has an international reputation for developing intelligent content strategies for multichannel delivery. She has been instrumental in establishing the field in content strategy, content reuse, intelligent content strategies for multichannel delivery, and structured content management best practices. Rockley is a frequent contributor to trade and industry publications and a keynote speaker at many conferences in North America, Europe, and Asia-Pacific.

Known as the "mother" of content strategy, she introduced the concept of content strategy with her ground-breaking book, *Managing Enterprise Content: A Unified Content Strategy*[44], now in its second edition. Ann is also the primary author of *Intelligent Content: A primer*, *DITA 101: Fundamentals of DITA for Authors and Managers*, and *eBooks 101: The Digital Content Strategy for Reaching Customers Anywhere, Anytime, on Any Device*. Ann is the creator of the concept of intelligent content and founded the Intelligent Content Conference.

Ann has a Master of Information Science from the University of Toronto and is a Fellow of the Society for Technical Communication. Ann is an adjunct professor at the Cork Institute of Technology, teaching Information Strategy in the MSc in Information Design and Development program.

Carmen Simon

Dr. Carmen Simon is a cognitive neuroscientist, author, and founder of Memzy, a company that uses brain science to help corporations create memorable messages. Carmen's book *Impossible to Ignore: Create Memorable Content to Influence Decisions*[48] has been selected as one of the top international books on persuasion. Carmen holds two doctorate degrees, and she also teaches at Stanford University. Dr. Simon holds frequent workshops for corporate audiences on the importance of using brain science to craft communication that is not only memorable but sparks action. After all, what's the use of memory if people don't act on it?

Val Swisher

Founder Val Swisher runs the content strategy, global content strategy, and content transformation service lines for Content Rules. Val has more than two decades of experience and is a well-known expert on global readiness, intelligent content, content development, and Acrolinx software. In her view, content should be easy to read, cost-effective to translate, and efficient to manage. Val is the author of three books: *Global Content Strategy: A Primer*[54], *Mastering Network Management*[53], and *The Comprehensive Guide to Computer Telephony Integration*[52]. Val is on the advisory board for the University of North Texas Technical Communications Program.

References and Further Reading

We use a link shortener in print because some of the links are extremely long. If you go to https://xmlpress.net/lec/references, you will find a list of references with the complete, un-shortened URL for each.

Cited References

[1] Abbey Communication. "What can native speakers of English do to improve international conference calls." https://xplnk.com/jrut0/

[2] Alive With Ideas "Guiding Non-Comms Colleagues Through Internal Comms Challenges." 2016. https://xplnk.com/hxfdj/

[3] Bailie, Rahel Anne. "Leveraging the Natural Connection Between ContentOps and Content Strategy." upland Kapost Blog. 2019. https://xplnk.com/gxiru/

[4] Barr, Stacey. "Why do YOU Measure Performance." November 15, 2011. https://xplnk.com/ft2to/

[5] Beheshti, Naz. "10 Timely Statistics About The Connection Between Employee Engagement and Wellness." Forbes.com. 2019. https://xplnk.com/rw41w/

[6] Bernoff, Josh. *Writing Without Bullshit.* Harper Business. 2016. https://xplnk.com/05mnq/

[7] Bernoff, Josh. "Bad Writing Costs Businesses Billions." The Daily Beast. 2017. https://xplnk.com/cc0ug/

[8] Burmark, Dr. Lynell. *Visual Literacy.* Assn for Supervision & Curriculum. 2002.

[9] Caplan, Bryan. "3 Reasons to Liven Up Your Marketing with Visual Content." Score. March 20, 2019. https://xplnk.com/5v09k/

[10] Catmull, Ed and Amy Wallace. *Creativity, Inc.* Random House. 2014. https://xplnk.com/rtbz3/

[11] Changing Minds. "Active Learning." Changing Minds. https://xplnk.com/pjvry/

[12] Clarine, Brenna. "11 Reasons Why Video is Better Than Any Other Medium." Advanced Web Ranking. https://xplnk.com/k0fcw/

[13] Cornell University. "The Negative Side of Cascading Information." Course blog for INFO 2040/CS 2850/Econ 2040/SOC 2090. https://xplnk.com/fil58/

[14] Delcker, Janosch. "Online photos can't simply be re-published, EU court rules." Politico. August 7, 2018. https://xplnk.com/my04m/

[15] DePhillips, Kari. "The $8,000 Mistake That All Bloggers Should Beware." The Content Factory. 2013. https://xplnk.com/fx8hj/

[16] Digital Signage Today. "Using Interactive Digital Signage to Increase Customer Engagement." Digital Signage Today. July 13, 2017. https://xplnk.com/zlf4d/

[17] Dranch, Konstantin. "Considering video game languages." Multilingual. May / June 2019.

[18] Dubois, David, Derek D. Rucker, and Adam D. Galinsky. "Understanding Power Dynamics Will Make You More Persuasive." Kellogg Insight. August 1, 2016. https://xplnk.com/cmar8/

[19] European Trade Union Institute (ETUI). "European Works Councils." European Trade Union Institute (ETUI). https://xplnk.com/vmc50/

[20] Foster, Daniel. "The Value of Visual Content and a Simplified User Interface." TechSmith. April 19, 2019. Content Wrangler webinar. https://xplnk.com/3verc/

[21] Gibson, Dr. Barbara. "Intercultural competencies needed by global CEOs." Birkbeck, University of London. 2014. PDF Format. PhD Thesis. https://xplnk.com/wylx8/

[22] Heid, Markham. "Does Thinking Burn Calories? Here's What the Science Says." Time Magazine. September 19, 2018. https://xplnk.com/25knb/

[23] hppy. "The Benchmark of Successful Internal Email Campaigns." 2018. https://xplnk.com/sspld/

References and Further Reading

[24] International Organization for Standardization (ISO). *Occupational health and safety, ISO 45001.* 2018. PDF format. A summary of the ISO 45001 standard. https://xplnk.com/uit5i/

[25] James, Geoffrey. "20 Epic Fails in Global Branding." Inc.com. 2014. https://xplnk.com/3zjs1/

[26] Klein, Mike. *The Present and Future of Internal Comms: How to measure what really matters.* happeo. Free download. The third of six reports. https://xplnk.com/pc199/

[27] Klein, Mike. *When hierarchy meets the world of influence…or, "Why do we keep getting asked to do cascades when we know they don't work?"* LinkedIn. August 23, 2018. The third of six reports for Happeo on the state of internal communications. https://xplnk.com/7wfwv/

[28] Kohl, John. *The Global English Style Guide: Writing Clear, Translatable Documentation for a Global Market.* SAS Press. 2008.

[29] Koivula, Juha. "Multilingual intranets: Automating your localization process with Microsoft Flow and Translator." Valo. February 2, 2018. https://xplnk.com/ajsty/

[30] Lamb, Brian, Fredrik Wackå, Audun Rundberg, and Gerry McGovern. "Intranet in a Box." Customer Carewords. 2015. https://xplnk.com/zu4bx/

[31] Levene, Abigail. "Beware the Photo Shoot." Stampa Communications. September 26, 2016. https://xplnk.com/7em4c/

[32] Lindsey, Jon Ann and Val Swisher. "Optimizing Content in the Real World at Google." LocWorld 35, Silicon Valley. November 2, 2017.

[33] Lum, Michael. "5 Scrum Meeting Best Practices: Master the Daily Stand-Up." Sprintly. March 2, 2016. https://xplnk.com/5a2gy/

[34] Mann, Annamarie and Jim Harter. "The Worldwide Employee Engagement Crisis." Gallup Workplace. 2016.

[35] Munter, Mary. "Cross-cultural communication for managers." Business Horizons, (Vol. 36, Issue 3). May 1, 1993. Detailed summary. Full paper available through Gale Academic Onefile. https://xplnk.com/n0frp/

[36] Ohlsen, Mark. *Insider's Guide to Translating Foreign Language Video.* LRS Recording. https://www.lrsrecording.com

[37] Ohlsen, Mark. *Insider's Guide To The Foreign Language Video Marketplace.* LRS Recording. https://www.lrsrecording.com

[38] Oldham, Cheryl A. "The Evolution of the Skills Gap Requires 21st Century Solutions." Forbes. March 4, 2019 https://xplnk.com/sgadq/

[39] Murphy, Jim. "How to Select the Intranet Foundation for Your Digital Workplace." Gartner. 2018. Available for purchase or for Gartner subscribers. https://xplnk.com/ua96l/

[40] Orwell, George. "Politics and the English Language." Horizon, (volume 13, issue 76, pages 252–265). April 1946. https://xplnk.com/m35gh/

[41] "Photography Copyright in Europe." Photoclaim. August 7, 2015.

[42] Power, Alan. "Creating a Design System Language." speckboy. 2017. https://xplnk.com/2uudi/

[43] Resolver. "What foreign companies need to know about SOX compliance." April 19, 2012. https://xplnk.com/rc63j/

[44] Rockley, Ann and Charles Cooper. *Managing Enterprise Content: A Unified Content Strategy,* Second Edition. New Riders: Voices That Matter, Pearson Education. 2012.

[45] Schlegel, Anna N. *Truly Global: The Theory and Practice of Bringing Your Company to International Markets.* FriesenPress. 2016.

[46] Schlegel, Anna N. "Grow Your Localization Career with Mentoring." Women in Localization Silicon Valley Chapter, May 3, 2018. Video presentation at the Women in Localization Silicon Valley Chapter meeting. https://xplnk.com/ga345/

[47] Schmidt, Will. "How to Orchestrate a Social Media Takeover from Scratch." Classy. https://xplnk.com/ga345/

[48] Simon, Carmen PhD. *Impossible to Ignore: Creating Memorable Content to Influence Decisions.* McGraw Hill. 2016.

[49] Strunk, William and E.B. White. *The Elements of Style.* Many editions exist.

[50] Suresh, Gokul. "Why Multi Billion-dollar Enterprises Are Adopting Interactive Walkthroughs in 2019." Whatfix. 2019. https://xplnk.com/f700h/

[51] Suresh, Swetha. "Design Language System." UX Planet. 2018. https://xplnk.com/pfes7/

[52] Swisher, Val. *The Comprehensive Guide to Computer Telephony Integration.* CT Institute.

[53] Swisher, Val. *Mastering Network Management.* Upper Access Book Pub. 1995. https://xplnk.com/mwzuu/

[54] Swisher, Val. *Global Content Strategy: A Primer.* XML Press. 2014. https://xplnk.com/ebu8x/

[55] Swisher, Val. "Three (Surprising) Reasons for Poor Quality Translations." LinkedIn. 2017. https://xplnk.com/y2f1e/

[56] Swisher, Val. "The Holy Trifecta: The Secret to Faster, Better, & Cheaper Global Content." Content Rules. 2017. https://xplnk.com/y83kl/

[57] Tien, Shannon. "How to Create a Social Media Content Calendar: Tips and Templates." Hootsuite. September 24, 2018. https://xplnk.com/eobnf/

[58] Vasileioy, Angelos. *Internal crisis communication and employee engagement: A closer look at multinational companies.* Lund University, Department of strategic communication. 2018. Master's thesis. https://xplnk.com/pqsle/

[59] *Digital Signage Guides,* Visix. A set of guides on topics related to digital signage. https://xplnk.com/r89k3/

[60] Walsh, Ray. "Jargon: Another Chance to Make it About You." LinkedIn. 2015. https://xplnk.com/e0b56/

[61] White, Martin. "Intranet Search Is More Than a Technology Problem." CMS Wire. 2018. https://xplnk.com/uq05v/

[62] Wickham, Natalie. "14 Benefits of Employee Engagement – Backed By Research." Quantum Workplace. April, 26, 2018. https://xplnk.com/2dd6g/

[63] Yunker, John. *Think Outside the Country: a Guide to Going Global and Succeeding in the Translation Economy.* Byte Level Books. 2017.

[64] Yunker, John. "What the best global websites have in common." Multilingual. May / June 2019. Preview issue. Subcription required to read the full article. https://xplnk.com/rbgog/

[65] Yunker, John. "The 2019 Web Globalization Report Card." Byte Level Research. 2019. https://xplnk.com/17cbr/

Additional reading

[66] Bosley, Deborah S. *Global Contexts: Case Studies in International Technical Communication.* First Edition Pearson. Part of the Allyn and Bacon Series on International Technical Communication.

[67] Harzing, Anne-Wil. "Language in International Business." Harzing. February 6, 2016 (updated July 13, 2019). https://xplnk.com/6py59/

[68] Harzing, Anne-Wil and Alan J. Feely. "The Language Barrier and its Implications for HQ-Subsidiary Relationships." Cross-cultural Management: An International Journal. 2007. PDF format. https://xplnk.com/3a5ov/

[69] Hofsted, Geert. *Culture's Consequences: International Differences in Work-Related Values,* 2nd edition. SAGE Publications. 2003. https://xplnk.com/rqa9v/

[70] Porter, Alan J. *The Content Pool.* XML Press. 2012. https://xplnk.com/gi6xk/

[71] Weiss, Edmond H. *The Elements of International English Style.* M.E. Sharpe. 2005.

Glossary

Active Directory
A Microsoft product that maintains a database of devices (computers, printers, storage, etc.) and users on a Windows domain network. It manages authentication, enforces security policies, and controls access to devices and information.

babies and birthdays
Idiomatic description among communications professionals to refer to the kind of content relevant only at a specific workplace, usually produced locally about human-interest events among colleagues.

brand
A sweeping term, sometimes defined as the overall experience with a specific product or offering. The concept of brand includes every aspect of a company's effort to distinguish a product from the competition. Often confused with the visual aspects brand identity, a brand includes not just a company or product name and logo, but also its reputation, positioning, the promise it makes to customers, its way of doing business, and more.

brand champion
Also known as a brand ambassador, someone who advocates for a brand and urges others to adopt it. In an internal context, brand champions encourage proper expression of the brand in all its aspects. For many companies brand champions are part of a formal program, with training and support from global marketing.

brand guidelines
A set of standards that describe how to express the brand. These standards are often shared with employees and vendors to prevent inconsistent use of brand identity elements. Such guidelines detail how to use the logo and other elements in documents, websites, trade-fair booths, equipment, and more, but they can also articulate abstract concepts—such as the desired personality for a brand or its promise/mission—and verbal aspects like voice and tone.

brand identity
Generally understood to be the visual elements of a brand, including its name, logo, tagline, and color palette, but a comprehensive identity can also include tone and voice and more. Most brand identities are a suite of visual elements created by professional designers, and the use of these elements is governed by a set of rules (see *brand guidelines*).

change management
A broad term describing actions companies take to help their employees through the process of change. Change management has emerged as its own business discipline, and its methodologies are often applied during mergers and acquisitions, new technology adoptions, new ways of working, relocations, or job losses. Change managers often work with Communications to create content related to the transition.

co-creation
A process where trained local communicators draw from shared visual and text assets to create content translated into their local language and modified to work well in their locale.

component content management system (CCMS)
A software application that manages content as re-usable components rather than fully finished documents. It can be paired with a traditional CMS. Components can be long blocks of content, but they are more likely to be re-usable assets such as a text paragraph, an image, or a definition. A CCMS provides structured content and can be combined with a terminology management system (TMS), machine translation, and translation memory tools to produce, adapt, manage, and deliver content in multiple languages.

content
Any text, image, video, decoration, or user-consumable elements that contribute to comprehension.

content management system (CMS)
A software application that supports information capture, editorial, governance, and publishing processes with tools such as workflow, access control, versioning, search, and collaboration.

content model
A formal representation of structured content as a collection of content types and their interrelationships.

corporate social responsibility (CSR)
A public disclosure mechanism of a company's ethical business practices. In recent years, public companies have begun issuing annual CSR reports in addition to, or integrated with, their annual earnings reports. CSR reports seek to explain the status of a company's relationships with various stakeholders, but especially among its employees and in the communities where it operates. Typical CSR reports include descriptions of activities and measurement of impact in three areas: community involvement, environmental impact, and evidence of behaving as a responsible employer.

DAM
Digital asset management. The process and technology used to store and manage digital assets such as images.

design system language
A single standard for designers to follow as they create and update deliverables. Although similar to traditional design guidelines, a DSL can also be a tool that designers use regardless of location. It includes not just standards but also assets and components from them to draw from. With the proliferation of channels and products in global organizations, a DSL can clarify brand standards for designers and anyone else responsible for visual treatment of a brand. A DSL is helpful in multiplying compliant expressions of a brand in internal systems, in managing local variety, and in transferring design knowledge to local business units.

design thinking
Design thinking originally described the preparation and processes that designers use to devise, propose, and create new products. In recent years it has also become synonymous with innovation and, as such, something of a movement. The term has been adopted by IT professionals and others who feel that process steps such as analyzing

context, discovering user behaviors and needs, and generating ideas also have relevance for their areas of work.

digital asset management
The process and technology used to store and manage digital assets such as images.

digital signage
LCD or LED displays mounted on walls or stands to provide visitors with up-to-the minute information, promotions, and directions. Multiple screens can be networked to facilitate the management and delivery of content. Digital signage systems are becoming increasingly sophisticated, with features such as user interactivity. In the workplace, digital signage can be used to reach employees in areas such as break rooms and reception areas.

editorial calendar
A schedule for the publishing of content over a given time period, often annually or during a given campaign period.

font family
A collection of related fonts. A font family may contain variants such as italics, bold, and bold italics. It may also contain versions optimized for larger print, such as titles, or smaller print. Some popular font families offer typefaces for non-Latin alphabets such as Arabic, and some have variants for non-alphabetic languages such as Chinese, Japanese, and Korean. Many corporations specify a font family for branded, external materials so that content has a consistent look and feel. Depending on the availability of that font in standard tools, they may also use it for internal communications.

General Data Protection Regulation (GDPR)
A European Union (EU) regulation designed to protect and ensure privacy of personal information for EU citizens. Although enforceable only in Europe, many global companies have overhauled their data management policies to comply with the GDPR. GDPR mostly applies to the storage and use of personal data, making it an IT and security issue. However, because photos of people are considered personal

data, GDPR also affects employee communications. Many companies require written consent (such as a *photo release*) from those depicted before a photo can be shared on internal web sites or social media.

glocal

A combination of globalization and localization, glocal means "reflecting or characterized by both local and global considerations" (according to Lexico.com,[1] powered by Oxford University Press). A communication in a local language that has both global key messages and local examples would be a glocalized communication.

Health and Safety (H&S)

H&S is an internal designation for activities focused on reducing and eliminating accidents at work and promoting general well-being among employees. Its methods are based on the multidisciplinary field of Occupational Health and Safety. Depending on the industry and region, practices and methodologies can be regulated by law, and companies often use their H&S measurements as part of their CSR reporting. H&S is typically a specialization that is overseen by the human resources department.

In-country review

A step in the content workflow, after translation and prior to publishing, where the content is reviewed by a person who is intimately familiar with the target audience—usually a person who lives and works for the client in the target market. That person does not have to be a professional translator.

Interpreting

The act of converting verbal (spoken or signed) communication from one language into another.

ISO 45001

According to ISO.org,[2] "ISO 45001 sets the minimum standard of practice to protect employees worldwide…ISO 45001 enables organizations to put in place an occupational health and safety (OH&S)

---

[1] https://www.lexico.com/en/definition/glocal
[2] https://www.iso.org/files/live/sites/isoorg/files/store/en/PUB100427.pdf

management system. This will help them manage their OH&S risks and improve their OH&S performance by developing and implementing effective policies and objectives."

localization

Adaptation of content to make it more meaningful, appropriate, and effective for a particular culture, locale, or market.

machine translation

A software-based process that translates content from one language to another.

material disclosure

A regulatory requirement governing any information that could affect a public company's stock price, such as earnings, changes in leadership, plant closings, etc. In 2000 the US Securities and Exchange Commission (SEC) began requiring companies to make market-sensitive information available to all parties at the same time, and requirements became more stringent two years later with the Sarbanes/Oxley legislation. Since employees are often stockholders, material disclosure requirements can affect how companies distribute material announcements internally.

metadata

Attributes of content you can use to structure, semantically define, and target content.

native speaker

Someone who has naturally used a language from an early age as a primary means of concept formation and communication rather than acquiring the language later in life.

network

The people in-country who help cascade and possibly adapt content for local audiences. In this context, *network* is an entirely human concept and has nothing to do with the company's technology systems. In many companies, network members are assigned locally and are not formally part of the communications department.

Glossary

photo release
A release form, signed by the people depicted in a photo or video, that details how the organization can use their image.

postmortem
Project managers borrowed the term from the medical profession, where it refers to a procedure to determine a person's cause of death. When used in a project management context, it means a formal assessment at the conclusion of a project about what was successful and what wasn't. Also known as lessons learned.

privileged information
Information that an organization considers confidential. Privileged information can remain within a limited group of people indefinitely, or it can remain privileged until the moment it is disseminated publicly (see *material disclosure*). For example, internal discussions about a proposed merger may be privileged to select executives and people in the legal and finance departments.

recognition
Formal or informal statements from management or peers that are meant to thank individuals or groups of employees for their work. Recognition can range from an informal thank you to a written letter to a formal program.

sketch
For designers, a sketch is a quick, visual rendering of a product or other deliverable. During the ideation phase of a project, it communicates the broad outlines of a concept. Designers use sketches to present concepts to clients and get early feedback.

storyboard
Originally referring to illustrations that depict a specific sequence in a film, the term has been adopted by businesses to describe early-stage efforts to develop presentations or design solutions. Analogous to a sketch, a storyboard proposes a sequence of slides for a presentation or the sequence of the user experience with a specific tool.

style guide
A set of guidelines and standards covering areas such as vocabulary, editing, tone, and voice. May extend to structural aspects of content.

town hall
A political tradition where a representative holds a meeting in a local town hall so that constituents can ask questions directly. Similarly, many corporations organize periodic meetings for large groups of employees to hear from and directly address corporate leadership. In the digital era, the meetings are often a mix of a live event with people in an auditorium combined with a videoconference option for employees in other locations.

translation
Conversion of content from one language to another.

translation memory
A repository that contains translated source and target language pairs. Used by human translators to speed translation and reduce costs by reusing previously translated content.

user-centered design
Also known as user-oriented design, a design framework that considers how, why, and in what circumstances users will experience a product. User-centered design researches user behavior to avoid having to train users or develop workarounds for design flaws. It is applied in many areas of business, including product design, technology, and tools.

wireframe
A schematic page layout, especially for proposed web content, depicting the interface and navigation. It is normally rendered without color, graphics, or typeface, focusing instead on functionality.

Workplace
Internal social-media platform developed by Facebook that enables informal collaboration and information sharing. The functionality mirrors that of other social media platforms, with groups, instant messaging, and posts that appear on user news feeds. Participation is normally limited to employees. Workplace is an example of an enter-

prise social network or social intranet. *Yammer* is a similar platform developed by Microsoft.

works council

A representative body of employees. Works councils are not unions; however, in many European countries, the works council must be consulted by management for any change in working conditions. Companies operating across several countries in the European Union must also maintain a European Works Council, an inter-country council.

Yammer

Internal social-media platform developed by Microsoft that enables informal collaboration and information sharing. The functionality mirrors that of other social media platforms, with groups, instant messaging, and posts that appear on user news feeds. Participation is normally limited to employees. Yammer is an example of an enterprise social network or social intranet. *Workplace* is a similar platform developed by Facebook.

Index

A

Acrolinx, 83, 122
acronyms, 49
action, inspiring, 5
Active Directory, 71
agencies
    budgeting when using, 143
    cost/benefit of using, 142
    guidelines for, 128
    importance of briefing, 142–146
    process for global businesses, 125
    social media, 170
    using to create content, 141–143
agile methodologies, 198
amateur photography, 147
anti-bribery policies, 33
Associated Press (AP) Stylebook, 121
audio
    in amateur videos, 148
    in conference calls, 139

B

babies and birthdays, 21, 190
backgrounders, marketing, 167
Bailie, Rahel Anne, 90, 176
Barr, Stacey, 162
barriers, technology, 30–31
Beautiful.AI, 91, 132
Bernoff, Josh, 38
Birt, Arlene, 47, 114, 148, **211**
born global companies, 67

Bosley, Deborah S., 38, 119, **211**
brand champions, 164
brand compliance, 14, 83, 102
    consistency versus flexibility, 125
    fixed versus flexible elements, 128
    images, 45
    reviews for, 99
    standards for, 79
brand identity, 14, 102, 148
    design system languages and, 129
    guidelines for visual, 183
    local contributions to, 160
    maintaining on social media, 169
    tone and voice, 186
brand management, models of, 77
brand refresh, 166
brand-related events, 24
branding missteps, 7
briefings, 145, 177
budget
    communications, 64–65
    translation, 113–115
    working with agencies, 143
budgeting time for review, 126
Burmark, Lynell, 50
business outcomes, measuring, 162
business writing, quality of, 37
business-unit metrics, 15

C

calendar
    editorial, 172, 198
    event, 189

campaign briefings, 105–107
Canva, 132
career development, 100, 180–182, 204
cascade, information, 11, 189
    required by law, 12
Catmull, Ed, xv, 175, 178, 191, 202
CCMS (*see* component content management system)
celebrations, 24
change management, 137, 144–145
chargebacks, 99
click rate, 7
Clipisode, 151
clusters, content, 20
CMS (*see* content management system)
co-creation, 85–86, 109, 116–117
    approaches to, 8–9
    templates and, 127
cognitive energy, 6
commercial rights, 45
communicating mission, 23
communication, visual, 43–50
Communications
    as a cost center, 59
    impact on revenue, 66
    reporting lines, 63
    staffing local, 15, 51–56
    working with marketing and sales, 167
community involvement, 192
company culture, 174
component content management system, 73
conference calls, 139–141
content, xiv
    corporate-generated, 22
    handcrafting, 159
    health and safety, 194–195
    holiday, 40
    insourced versus outsourced, 143
    issues with outsourced, 142
    locally generated, 21
    measuring localized, 160
    outsourcing, 141
    reviews, 190
    silos, 159
    using agencies to create, 141–143
content clusters, 20
content management system, 45
    as a DAM, 153
    component, 73
content models, 160
content reuse, 159–168
    organizational barriers to, 159
content strategy, 176
context, providing local, 22
contingent workers, 31
contractors, 31
corporate culture, 137
    pride and, 193
corporate social responsibility, 93, 192
corporate storytelling, 23
cost center, Communications as a, 59
crisis management, 61–62
crowd-sourced video, 49
cultural bias
    combatting, 138
    images, 45
cultural blindness, 173
cultural competency, 181
cultural references, 17, 118
    visual communication and, 43
cultural reinforcers, 95
culture
    corporate, 137
        pride and, 193
    fundraising and, 192
    recognition and, 193
    tone and voice and, 186
    volunteering and, 192

D

DACH, 56
data distortion, 28
decentralized localization models, 78

Index 235

demographics
　employee, 27
　social media, 172
design system language, 129–130
design thinking, 126
design, user-centered, 80
designers
　connecting with users, 125–126
destination intranet, 69, 208
digital asset management system, 44, 153
digital signage, 147–158
　interactive, 157
　local, 154–156
　maintaining, 156
disclosure requirements, 12
distributed intranet, 69
document management
　privileged information and, 12
Dranch, Konstantin, 105
dubbing video, 47

E

E1 and E2 English, 118
editorial calendar, 172, 198
educational opportunities, 180
email, localizing, 105
emotional connection, 173
employee deliverables, graphing, 25
employee demographics, 27
employee engagement, 10
employee recognition, 193
　(*see also* recognition)
engagement, 8
　consequences of low, 10, 61
　employee, 10
　employee demographics and, 27
　employee recognition and, 161
　human resources and, 10
　measuring, 75
　reader, 7
English
　as a corporate language, 4

E1 and E2 speakers, 118
　US versus UK, 123
　used to inform, 103
English-only content
　alternatives to, 9
　intranet, 7
enterprise search, 75
Europe, workplace conditions in, 55
event calendar, 189
external staff, 31

F

feedback, user, 127
firewalls, internal, 28
fluency, 13
Foster, Daniel, 44, 115
four-language test, 176
franchise partners, 32
fundraising, cultural considerations, 192

G

Gartner Group, 69, 180
General Data Protection Regulation, 150
Germany, workplace conditions in, 55
Gibson, Barbara, 67, 138–139, 181, **211**
global content strategy, 176
glocal, 22
glocal hybrids, 25
glossaries, 41
Google Image Search, 151
Google Translate, 119, 123
Grammarly, 151
graphics
　making adaptable, 125–134
　managing, 46–47
graphing employee deliverables, 25
guidelines
　localization, 130–133
　visual element, 132

H

habits, 6
Halfhead, Rosie, 68–69, 102, 166, 180, **211**
handcrafting content, 159
health and safety, 194–195
Hofsted, Geert, 138
holiday content, 40
holiday references, 16, 189
Holy Trifecta, 73, 90
human resources
    engagement and, 10
humor, 49

I

idiomatic versus plain language, 118
image bank, 45
image subscription service, 45
images
    cliché, 184
    cultural concerns, 152
    health and safety issues in, 178
    inappropriate, 152
    metadata, 44–45, 153
in-country reviews, 33, 39, 101–102, 116, 174
industry publications, 180
informants, 51
information cascade, 11
    required by law, 12
informing, versus persuading, 23
    language choice for, 103–105
innate reinforcers, 5
Instagram, 171
intellectual property laws, 151
intelligent content, 62
interactive digital signage, 157
interfaces
    localizing, 114–115
internal content, mistaken for external, 125
internal firewalls, 28
international mindset, 138
interpreting, 116
intranet
    English-only, 7, 70
    improving your, 69
    local language, 71
    metrics, 73
    multilingual, 70
ISO 45001, 195

J

jargon, 186
Jazz Hands content, 118
jokes, 118
Just the Facts content, 118

K

key performance indicators, 15, 145, 157
Klein, Mike, 75, 163
Klingon, 184
Kohl, John, 122, **212**

L

labor issues, 12
language, 4
    (*see also* English)
    (*see also* local language)
language service provider (LSP), 62
leadership meetings, 24
leadership videos, 22
legal issues
    cascades required by, 12
    contractor-related, 31–32
    images, 45, 149
Lindsey, Jon Ann, 71
local language
    social media, 170
    used to persuade, 103
localization, 13
    centralized vs. decentralized, 78
    guidelines for, 130–133

Index   237

justifying the need for, 60
measuring success of, 160
models, 77–92
scenario-based, 113
tying to business outcomes, 68
localizing video, 38, 47, 49
low engagement, consequences of, 10

M

Maas, Élise LeMoing, 173–175, **212**
machine translation, 35, 73, 119–121
    accuracy of, 115
    employee acceptance of, 115
    in-country review of, 101
management style, 202
market-by-market rollouts, 181
marketing backgrounders, 167
marketing content, sharing, 166
markets, resources in different sized, 53
Mars rover
    Corporate Communications and, 3
material information, 12, 72
Matthews, Sean, 155, 157, **212**
McGovern, Gerry, 70, 72, 74, 76, **213**
measurement, 26
    (*see also* metrics)
measurement workshops, 201
meetings
    conference calls, 139–141
    scheduling, 198
    team, 197–201
    translators for, 199
memory, short and long-term, 50
mentoring, 187
messaging briefs, 177
metadata
    image, 44–45, 153
    search, 71, 76
metrics, 26
    audience preference, 161
    business unit, 15, 162
    comparing different countries', 201

cost/benefit of using agencies, 142
intranet, 73
local considerations, 26
search, 76
micromanaging, 175
mindset, international, 138
mission, communicating, 23
models
    brand management, 77
    decentralized localization, 78
    localization, 77–92
mother tongue, 5
multilingual intranets, 70
Munter, Mary, 138

N

narration speed, 48
native speakers, 40
network, xiv, 51
    building, 66
    Corporate Communications and its, 64–65
    developing your, 197–205
    working with your, 183–195
network of work, 69
news, local versus global, 27
newsfeeds, in digital signage, 157
non-employee workforce, 31
Nuxio, 153

O

off-site meetings, 197
official language, English as the, 4
Ohlsen, Mark, 38, 48–49, 116, 148, **213**
Oram, Alan, 125, 167, 172, **213**
Orwell, George, 37
outsourced content, 141
    issues with, 142
outsourced labor, 31

P

Pachinko, 13
page views, 75
performance measures
    employee, 61
    persuading, versus informing, 23
        language choice for, 103–105
Phillips, Jonathan, 12, 70, 72, 162, 191, **213**
photo library, 149
    limitations, 152
photo release, 147
photography, 147–158
    amateur, 147
    health and safety issues in, 178
    legal issues, 149
    managing, 44
plagiarism, 151
plain language, 37, 117–119
    idiomatic language versus, 118
planning calendar, 176
pop culture references, 16
Porter, Alan J., 45, 153, **214**
posters, safety, 23, 194
postmortems, 29, 191
Power, Alan, 129
preferred vendors, 32
Prezi, 91, 132
pride, company, 193
privacy regulations, 28
privileged information, 12
    document management and, 12
problems, collaborating to solve, 202
production timelines, 24
professional development (*see* career development)
proficiency, English, 7
Promo, 151
ProWritingAid, 151
publications, industry, 180

Q

Qordoba, 122
qualitative data, collecting, 28–30
quantitative data, collecting, 26–28

R

Ragan, 180
Rau, Leonard, 4, 46, 137, 164–166, **214**
re-branding, 117
re-purposing content (*see* content reuse)
read rate, 7
readability, 48
reader engagement, 7
recognition, 23, 161
    cultural considerations, 193
references
    cultural, 118
reflexes, 6
regulations
    privacy, 28
regulatory issues, 11
reinforcers, 5
    cultural, 95
    primary, 95
    secondary, 5
release, photo, 147
repository
    image, 44
requests, deflecting low-value, 180
return on investment, Communications, 60
reuse, content, 159–168
    organizational barriers to, 159
reviews
    brand compliance, 99
    content-in-progress, 190
    importance of budgeting time for, 126
    in-country, 33, 39, 101–102, 116, 174
    user, 126
Rockley, Ann, 62, 133, 159–160, **214**
rollouts, market-by-market, 181

S

safety campaigns, 21
safety posters, 194
scheduling meetings, 198
Schlegel, Anna, 187
Schmidt, Will, 171
SCRUMs, 199
search
    enterprise, 75
secondary reinforcers, 5
sensory memories, 5
shout outs, 16
signage
    digital, 147–158
    digital, interactive, 157
    digital, maintaining, 156
silos, 35, 159
Simon, Carmen, 5, 11, 95, **215**
site visits, 188
slang, 49
social media, 169–172
    demographics, 172
    local-language, 170, 172
    teams, working with, 170
sports analogies, 16
staffing, 15
stock photos
    corporate, 46
storytelling, 161, 185
    social media, 171
    weaving messaging into, 177
storytelling, corporate, 23
structured content, 73
Strunk, William, 37
style
    translation, 36
style guides, 121–123
    automated tools, 122
subscription service, image, 45
subtitling video, 47
Suresh, Swetha, 130
surprise initiatives, 145

Swisher, Val, xv, 8, 38, 45, 71, 73, 90, 97, 117, 152, 169, 173, 175, **215**

T

take-action rate, 7
taxonomy, 153
team building, 173–132, 187
team meetings, 197–201
technology barriers, 30–31
templates, 80, 126
    allocating space in, 131
    co-creation and, 127
    importance of easy-to-use, 15
    library of, 127, 151
    localizing with, 130–133
    new technologies for, 91–92
terminology management system, 73
Tien, Shannon, 176
time references, 97
time, budgeting for review, 126
tone and voice, 186–187
Top Tasks Management, 74
town hall meetings, 22, 144
training, 199–201
translation
    allocating budget for, 113–115
    approaches to, 8–9
    as a commodity, 40
    assessing the cost of, 40
    assessing the quality of, 110–112
    bad writing and, 38
    challenges, 35–42
    cost of internal, 39–42
    machine, 35, 73, 119–121
        accuracy of, 115
        employee acceptance of, 115
        in-country review of, 101
    managing, 109–124
    user experience and, 113
    word-for-word, 36
translation vendors, 109

U

Unified Content Strategy, 159
unions, 137
unions versus works councils, 202
usability
    language as a barrier to, 7
user experience
    as a factor in budgeting, 113
user-centered design, 80
    importance of user input, 126

V

values
    communicating, 23
    management support of, 202
vendors
    translation, 109
    using to create content, 141
video, 147–158
    amateur, 148
    crowd-sourced, 49
    dubbing vs. subtitles, 48
    employee-produced, 49
    health and safety issues in, 178
    legal issues, 149
    local, 151
    localizing, 38, 47, 49
    managing, 47–50
    talking-head, 47
video cuts, 48
VisibleThread, 122
vision, communicating, 23
visual brand, 14, 183
visual communication, 43–50
voice, tone and, 186
volunteering, cultural considerations, 192

W

webinars, 144
White, E.B., 37
White, Martin, 75
Women in Localization, 187
word-for-word translation, 36
Workplace by Facebook, 208
works councils, 30, 55–56
    unions versus, 202
workshops, 199–201
    measurement, 201
writing
    quality of business, 37

Y

Yammer, 208
Yunker, John, 30, 77, 110, 112, 139, 174

Colophon

About the Author

Ray Walsh is an American content consultant based in Prague. A one-time journalist, English language teacher, and later employee communications manager, he has broad experience in content creation for various industries in settings that include global multinationals based in the US and Europe. He has worked in Belgium, Germany, and the Czech Republic for more than 15 years.

About the Content Wrangler Content Strategy Book Series

The Content Wrangler Content Strategy Book Series from XML Press provides content professionals with a road map for success. Each volume provides practical advice, best practices, and lessons learned from the most knowledgeable content strategists in the world. Visit the companion website for more information contentstrategybooks.com.

About XML Press

XML Press (xmlpress.net) was founded in 2008 to publish content that helps technical communicators be more effective. Our publications support managers, social media practitioners, technical communicators, and content strategists and the engineers who support their efforts.

Our publications are available through most retailers, and discounted pricing is available for volume purchases for educational or promotional use. For more information, send email to orders@xmlpress.net or call us at (970) 231-3624.

www.ingramcontent.com/pod-product-compliance
Lightning Source LLC
Chambersburg PA
CBHW070547160426
43199CB00014B/2406